Armgard and Sisi Michelet

DANCING ON A VOLCANO

The Michelet Sisters from 1914 - 1945

Laila Embelton

Red
Book

First published in Great Britain by Red Book, 2011
Copyright © Laila Embelton 2011
laila@bigpond.net.au

ISBN 978-1-4476-2910-8

The Red House Yarmouth Road Melton Woodbridge IP12 1QE

3/111001

ACKNOWLEDGEMENTS

Without the help and advice of my cousin Edzard this book could never have been written. He has supported my efforts over these last years, armed me with information about his parents, corrected my errors and taught me that truth, like humanity, is always complex. Wherever I have written my own opinions, he has accepted them for what they are – whether or not he entirely agrees with them. There is no doubt that Edzard suffered greatly, both during and after the war, yet he has had the strength to accept the past and be hopeful about the future.

Magnus, my son, has been a tower of strength to me, goading me into finishing the manuscript so that this story could be brought to the printed page. He also used one of his many talents to design the cover.

Where Noble family history is concerned, it is my brother Tim on whom I have leant for advice. I thank him for reading my manuscript, offering extra anecdotes and suggestions, and correcting any faults he encountered along the way.

And I cannot leave out my husband George, who has patiently accepted my need to spend so much time on this venture and who has encouraged and helped me every step of the way.

Knyphausen

von Benda

Graf Unico zu Innhausen
und Knyphausen
1831-1901

Julia
Mendez-Seixas

Kurt von
Lambrecht-Benda
1848-1922

Miriam
Gentz
1863-1947

Graf Franz
Knyphausen
1866-1958

Ida Mertens
Rauch
1870-1941

Ingeborg (Omi)
von Lambrecht-Benda
1884-1966

Graf Anton
Knyphausen
1905–1997

Armgard
Michelet
1909– 2004

Graf Edzard
Knyphausen
1935-

Michelet

Noble

Johan (August)
Michelet
1844-1926

Sophie
Steenstrup
1850-1936

Sir Andrew
Noble
1831-1915

Margery
Campbell
1828-1929

Johan
Michelet
1877 - 1964

Sir John
Noble
1865-1938

Amie (Darling)
Waters
1879-1973

Sigrid (Sisi)
Michelet
1911-2001

Sir Andrew (Paddy)
Noble
1904-1987

Sir Iain
Noble
1935-2010

Laila Noble
(Embelton)
1937-

Sir Timothy
Noble
1943 -

NOTE ON EMBASSIES AND LEGATIONS

In the mid-sixteenth century the Emperor Charles V ordained that the word ambassador should be applied only to the representatives of crowned heads and the then very weighty Republic of Venice. Minor states were not to use this term; their representatives should be called ministers.

In later centuries legations became the usual diplomatic mission, headed by ministers. Embassies were only exchanged between two major powers.

Since the Second World War the word legation has gradually been dropped. All countries now have ambassadors in embassies – except British Commonwealth countries, which exchange high commissioners.

CONTENTS

1

A Reunion 1987

As I walked through her front door I sensed she had news for me. Since she was never one to blurt out the thoughts that lay uppermost in her mind, this was obviously going to be a waiting game. Over the years I had learnt to understand my mother, to know when something pleased or displeased her, or when she was facing a problem she didn't feel equipped to handle.

We started with a few chores that needed my help. Before long she checked her watch and headed for the drinks tray. Pouring herself a sizeable whisky, she settled on the sofa, inviting me to join her. She never drank whisky before my father died but now it seemed to bring some kind of comfort, easing her loneliness and helping to subdue her very real grief.

We chattered aimlessly, as though killing time. Placing her empty glass on the table in front of her, she watched the sun drift behind a row of London terraced houses, leaving as its finale a sky the colour of crushed strawberries. I wondered if she was remembering happy days in China or sunsets on the beach in Brazil.

But she had other things on her mind. 'My sister's coming to stay next week.'

'Do you mean Armgard?' It was an unnecessary question because she only had one sister, but I was so astonished by her statement that the words tumbled out.

She said nothing, but it didn't take a mind reader to notice she was full of apprehension.

'Why didn't she come and stay before?' I asked, searching for a way into her thoughts.

'She just didn't'.

'It would have been nice for you – for all of us. Did you invite her?'

'She didn't have much money. It was … well, it wasn't easy.'

I took a deep breath. 'Had you quarrelled?'

'Oh no, nothing like that. It's …', she thought for a moment, 'it's just the way it was.'

I looked around her sitting room. On the walls hung portraits of my father's parents and a large oil painting of his family home in Scotland. Here and there, perched on shelves or scattered on pieces of antique furniture, were framed photographs of my father's relatives, also of my brothers and me, and our children.

But none of Armgard. There never have been.

'My sister will take a bus from the airport because I know you're working that day', my mother was saying. 'She won't have much luggage. She's only staying a few days.'

My sister. My sister. Why did she speak of Armgard as though she needed to be kept at arm's length? And why have I never thought to ask questions before? Driving home that evening, I scrolled through my memory for information about Armgard. I knew she lived in Switzerland because my mother once visited her, staying at their summer house overlooking Lake Maggiore. No stories or snippets of gossip emerged after that visit, just banal answers to my questions and descriptions of the view from the window. Of course I should have pressed her to divulge more while it was still fresh in her memory. My father was still alive at that time and might have added to the conversation by discussing Armgard as he remembered her, or at least giving me some clue as to why he had not also made the trip to Switzerland.

As it was I had little information. I knew that Armgard and my mother were the only children of a Norwegian diplomat. Their German mother's family once owned extensive properties and farms in Prussia. I often heard stories about the sisters' peripatetic childhood and was shown photographs of them holidaying in Germany, then living in China and Brazil, where their father's diplomatic career had taken them.

Four years before the start of the Second World War, Armgard married a German journalist, Graf (Count) Anton zu Knyphausen und Innhausen, giving up her Norwegian passport to become a

German citizen – as was expected of wives in those days.

Soon afterwards my mother married Paddy (Andrew) Noble, my father. Like his father-in-law before him, Paddy was a career diplomat and also served in China where, in December 1941 my parents, my brother and I were captured in Shanghai by the Japanese. When we returned to Britain, a year after that ordeal had started, Paddy was chosen to work on the Joint Intelligence Staff (JIS) in Churchill's inner sanctum, the Cabinet War Rooms.

He was well chosen for the job, being both a staunch patriot and a master of discretion. He had good reason, even during his childhood, for keeping himself to himself. However, it was time spent working in the Cabinet War Rooms that honed his art of verbal camouflage to perfection. Long after the war, when interesting snippets of information were being drip-fed to a hungry readership, he was often asked about his work on the JIS. Years of being drilled into a state of total secrecy about his job still controlled his thinking. 'I am bound by the Official Secrets Act', he would say, and carefully change the subject.

Sometimes friends probed further, hoping for an intriguing nugget, but he always managed to parry their questions with a throw-away remark such as: 'Once, when we were at our busiest, I was at my desk on Christmas Day. The canteen came up trumps; they served roast turkey and a glass of wine.'

Now, more than forty years after the end of the war, Armgard was coming to visit my mother. I would be able to talk to my aunt and discover why she had been virtually excluded from my life so far.

But it was never going to be as easy as that.

Armgard and my mother came from a family, and of a generation, who believed that withholding emotions was tantamount to good manners. My every effort to unearth clues to explain the rift was always hampered by one or other of them. When Armgard and I managed to spend time on our own, she dominated the conversation by asking about my family and my interests. As we walked through Kensington Gardens, watching children sail their model boats on the Round Pond, I gradually steered the conversation back towards her only son, Edzard, and his children and then, as tactfully as possible, drew her back into the past.

'During the war, when Edzard was still a small child, you lived in Berlin. That must have been very hard for you?'

She slowed her pace to almost a standstill, looking beyond the trees into space as though space were time and time might deflect my curiosity. I waited, easing my pace to coincide with hers. After a while she turned to me. 'Those of us who lived through such terrible years prefer to forget.'

There were so many questions to ask – so much family history to learn. And yet, for the time being, I had no choice but to respect her silence. It was two years later that I finally sat down to talk with her in her own home and gradually, year by year, won enough trust for her to begin the long task of unburdening her story to me. I should say most of her story, because parts of it, as I would discover, remained veiled behind an interwoven web of well-practised half-truths that she had created over the years to diffuse questions about her life during the latter part of the war.

When we were children, Armgard's name was seldom mentioned in our home. As far as I could tell she barely existed in my parents' thoughts. There was one occasion, however, on which my father spoke of her and, perhaps because they were so unexpected, his words remained clearly in my mind. I was setting out for my first grown-up party and he was ready, as always, with a compliment, admiring my new dress and first pair of high-heeled shoes. Then his voice changed. 'What a pity', he murmured, 'you don't have beautiful auburn hair like your Aunt Armgard'. His eyes had a faraway look that even then disturbed me, yet instead of awakening some sense of curiosity, his words merely strengthened the barrier in my mind between our happy Scottish family and unknown relations from Germany. In those days the notion that Allies were heroes and Germans were our enemy still had me firmly in its grasp.

Forty-five years later Armgard's visit awakened my curiosity, but my father was no longer alive to answer my many questions. I felt frustrated at every turn. Faced with such a blanket of secrecy at home, I thought of other ways to garner information: perhaps a phone call to Norway would be useful. Harriet Michelet, Armgard's and my mother's cousin, had stayed with my parents in London several times. When I finally caught her at home, I asked Harriet if my mother ever talked about Armgard.

'No', she said. 'It's strange. She told me Armgard lived in Switzerland now but never mentioned anything about the war. And no, she didn't explain why they hardly ever saw each other.

Not on any one of my visits. I didn't like to ask too much; I assumed that one day she'd feel ready to talk me about it of her own accord ... but she never has.'

Not long after Armgard's visit my husband, Kenneth Spence, was diagnosed with a virulent form of leukaemia. My three children and I concentrated all our thoughts on him, admiring his courage and determination as he attempted to outmanoeuvre his enemy.

It was many months after his untimely death the following year that my search for answers to the wartime enigma drew my attention once more. My brother Iain made one of his periodic visits to London from his home on the Isle of Skye, and over dinner we talked at length about our parents. 'I never mentioned this to you before but, just before she died, Daisy confided to me that Armgard's husband came to England during the war, hoping to broker a peace deal.'

Daisy was a close friend of my father's family and a much-loved confidante of both my parents. 'Did you ask Daddy about that?'

'Yes', Iain told me. 'He was rather taken aback by my question and gave me only a brief answer. I remember his words exactly. He confirmed that Knyphausen came to Britain, offering to give Churchill information about Hitler's plans; there was great uncertainty about whether he had come as a spy or a friend, so he never saw Churchill and was quickly sent back.'

The next day we confronted my mother with this fragment of family history.

'Who told you that? Pay no attention to any of it. No, I don't know anything about what my sister's husband did during the war. It was all so long ago and it doesn't really matter any more now, does it. She married again after the war was over, you know. He's Swiss.'

My mother offered nothing more on the subject of Knyphausen, but I persevered: 'Did you like him? You went to their wedding, didn't you – and you once told me you visited them in Berlin before the war.'

'I suppose so, but it was all such a long time ago and I don't think about those days any more. There's no point. I prefer remembering the happy times when I was married and you were young and ...'

'But did you like Armgard's husband?'

'I can't remember him really.'

Was it so much easier to bury the past than confront it?

Nor was my father of any help; his memoirs failed to mention Armgard or her husband, and their names never appeared in any of the letters he kept. And long after others involved in British wartime intelligence had written books about their work or the politics of war, my father remained silent. He never divulged secrets.

2

Stötterlingenburg 1914-18

After her visit to my mother, Armgard invited me to stay at her home in Switzerland. Nearly two years later I made the first of many visits to Basel. Sitting comfortably in her small flat, we whiled away the hours with talk about the past. Her English was excellent, coloured with a German accent and an American intonation left over from the school she attended in China. How different she sounded from my mother, who had over the years adopted an English accent, complete with intonations and phraseology that even Professor Higgins would have found difficult to distinguish from the voices of London ladies in whose houses she dined. My father used to say she was one of the very few foreigners he ever met who could pass as a British person, despite being nurtured in other languages.

In Basel I began by plying Armgard with questions about her youth, knowing that on this matter she felt herself to be on safe ground and would speak freely. Each evening I scribbled notes into a series of exercise books, slowly slotting together the jigsaw puzzle of her childhood – a childhood that would influence decisions she made later in life.

'Tell me about the First World War. Didn't you and my mother go to Germany at some stage?'

'Yes,' she told me, 'we were living in Paris and left on a train at the end of July 1914 to have a short holiday with my grandparents in Germany.'

'Wasn't that a little unwise, under the circumstances?'

'Perhaps it was a mistake. It ruined my parents' marriage. But for my mother it seemed the right thing to do at the time. She wasn't well. She was frequently short of breath and thought a holiday with her parents in the Harz Mountains would do her good.'

'Didn't she realise the war was about to start?'

'My father told her he read in the Norwegian newspaper that, although there were rumours of Germany preparing for war, nothing could happen for at least a few more weeks because the Kaiser was still holidaying on his yacht in Norway. Of course he never wanted my mother to go away and leave him on his own for two weeks; he really loved her then. But my grandmother sent money for the tickets and that was that.'

'Why didn't he join you for the holiday?'

'He couldn't. He was a diplomat who had only just been posted to the Norwegian Legation in Paris. He was thrilled with his appointment. As you know, his antecedents came from France; he was proud to be one of the Michelet family. He spoke fluent French and had read lots of French literature. Ever since they were married it had been his ambition to bring my mother to live in Paris – and he achieved it. He hoped to have a son one day who would be born in France and carry his name. But it never happened.'

Johan and Ingeborg (Omi) Michelet

She paused for a while. 'I'll tell you the whole story.'

As she talked, I remembered the few brief holidays we spent at the home of my maternal grandparents when I was still in my early teens. We called my grandmother 'Omi', short for Omama – the German word for Granny. Sometimes Omi would sit beside me on the sofa with a photograph album stretched across our two laps. Those black and white images of her childhood home in Germany became the visual foundation on which her stories still lodge in my mind. As Armgard reminisced in her flat in Basel, Omi's long-ago stories came back into focus and merged into Armgard's narrative as though it were all one stream of thought.

'I remember the journey well.' Armgard was saying. 'My mother had brought scrapbooks and coloured pencils to occupy the time until we reached Berlin.'

Armgard, six years old, helped her younger sister colour the pages. When they bid farewell to their father at the Gare du Nord in Paris, the girls were still speaking Norwegian, but as his forlorn figure faded from view behind a cloud of soot spewed out by the departing engine, they remembered, halfway through a sentence, to change into German, their mother-tongue. This was the language in which they felt at ease, the language they spoke when they were alone with their mother. It was the language of fun and laughter, of games played on the floor with dice and of their mother's soothing voice in the evenings when she read fairy stories to send them to sleep.

The first delay occurred after the train crossed the border from Belgium into Germany. An official came to inspect their credentials. Omi handed over her Norwegian diplomatic passport, with the names of Armgard and Sisi hand-written beside hers. The inspector bowed obsequiously before moving through the carriage, checking tickets and passports. He clambered down onto the platform and walked away. The train stayed put. Then, just as Armgard and Sisi began to think they would die of boredom, the engine, spitting and coughing, jolted into action. At the same time a train, recently arrived from the opposite direction, came to a halt on the far side of the station. As their own engine gradually gathered speed on its journey towards Berlin, all eyes turned to watch as the newly arrived train threw open its doors to disgorge a seemingly never-ending stream of soldiers.

A heavy silence filled the carriage.

The train steamed on peacefully through the Ruhr Valley until a cacophony of squealing brakes announced it was pulling into a siding. Soon afterwards a series of trains, one close on the tail of the next, whistled past them in the opposite direction. Nobody spoke. Even the girls, watching their mother closely, remained quiet. Omi was struggling to control her breathing, her mind entirely focused on taking long slow gulps of air as the doctor had instructed. As though there was not enough air in the whole world to fill her lungs. As though the world was turning upside down inside her body.

After a while the girls lost count of the number of trains heading for the Belgian border. But there was no mistaking one thing: every one of them was filled to overflowing with the Kaiser's troops. Thousands upon thousands of them.

By the time they reached Stötterlingenburg House and the enveloping arms of the entire von Lambrecht-Benda family, Armgard and Sisi were too tired to complain when their mother was swept away to lie in a darkened room. Her coughing had grown so frequent that she could barely whisper good night to them.

Miriam von Lambrecht-Benda, their grandmother, took charge of the girls. Every afternoon they played quietly in the *salon* while the adults listened to the wireless. The newsreader recited from the script with obvious relish. Their grandfather snorted approval. Although they had no understanding of what was happening, the girls enjoyed the atmosphere. But when, a short while later, the Kaiser ordered his troops to march into Belgium, and even Britain declared war on Germany, their mother wept until her whole body shook and the coughing began all over again. They could find no way to soothe her.

Even Miriam was only modestly successful at calming her eldest daughter. She explained, quietly but firmly, what she had read in the newspapers: the French and Russians had ganged up on Germany and therefore the Kaiser had no choice but to put them in their place. Since the German Army was far superior to the French and British – and better prepared – the war would be over in a month or two.

And then, only a day or two later, a worse calamity occurred.

Miriam called for the girls and asked them to join her in the *salon*, where the family doctor stood centre stage, his back to the empty fireplace. His face wore a grim expression. He waited until

Armgard and Sisi had lodged themselves close to one another on the sofa before he started to talk.

Their mother, he told them, was not well. She had contracted tuberculosis. Since tuberculosis is a contagious disease, he had arranged for her to be admitted to one of Germany's best sanatoriums where, in time, she would probably be cured. He paused to let the impact of what he said sink in. Then he turned to Miriam. Using a voice that somehow managed to be both deferential and authoritative at the same time, he advised her to order a carriage to transport her daughter to the sanatorium as soon as possible.

After their mother's departure the girls wandered around the house hand-in-hand, trying to bring each other comfort and learning to cope with the prospect of life without her. They longed for her warmth and familiarity. Though the von Lambrecht-Benda family was well meaning and Miriam spent many hours talking and reading to the girls, it seemed nothing would fill the gap in their lives. Their hearts ached for the one person who understood their every mood.

As war pitilessly spread its battlefields like a spilt bottle of red ink across the map of Europe, travel became impossible. Their summer holiday extended into autumn and soon it seemed as though the seasons had melted one into the other. Under the caring eye of Miriam, they gradually settled into their new life.

In Paris, Johan carried on his work at the Legation. During the weeks following the declaration of war, the streets were hung with huge posters calling for '*Mobilisation Générale*'. Insults to the Kaiser were chanted relentlessly by mobs marching down the Grands Boulevards. Paris, the city Johan loved so much, was changing before his eyes.

'In France', he read in the newspaper, 'there are only two classes of citizens: those who are leaving to fight the invading *Boche* and those who are looking after the soldiers of tomorrow.' His wife and daughters were now separated from him by more than just distance and there were rumours that the fighting would last for many months.

Meanwhile, at Stötterlingenburg House Armgard and Sisi started a new regime. Each morning they headed for the schoolroom to join the classes given by a governess to their youngest aunt, Feechen (barely six years older than Armgard) and her friend Trudchen, who lived in a neighbouring house. Feechen resented the inroads her nieces made into her comfortable position as the youngest member of the family, so Armgard and Sisi quickly learnt to avoid her company whenever possible and ran instead to find their oldest – and by now favourite – aunt, Tante Sigrid, after whom Sisi was named. It was Armgard who bestowed the nickname on her sister soon after her birth in Oslo, a name that she retained for the rest of her life. Tante Sigrid, on the other hand, was born at Stötterlingenburg and, apart from a few visits to her parents' small apartment in Berlin, had lived nowhere else. Although she was already twenty, and therefore a grown-up, she found time to run hand-in-hand with her nieces through the garden, out past the tennis court and on into the fields, where they watched farm workers trampling on the beet to extract sugar.

Stötterlingenburg House

When autumn showers made outdoor activities impossible, the three of them dashed round the house counting bedrooms.

'Fourteen', shouted Sisi gleefully, having first conferred with Armgard.

'Wrong', laughed her aunt. 'There are sixteen. See if you can find two more.'

Sometimes their grandfather took them for rides in his pony trap. It made them feel important to sit beside him while he toured his estate, stopping to talk to villagers or watching the farm workers gather in the rye. He also instructed them on the history of the area, Saxony-Anhalt, which was still a part of the Prussian empire, and told them about the building of Stötterlingenburg:

17

the house was designed by the architect Martin Gropius, a man of great vision and an eye to the future – he even installed a bathroom in the house alongside the bedrooms. His great nephew was to become yet more famous as the founder of the Bauhaus in Weimar.

Armgard and Sisi soon learnt to stop asking Miriam when their mother would return, knowing the answer would be too vague to lift their spirits. Occasionally Omi re-appeared at Stötterlingenburg for the weekend, and then made farewells on Monday morning as her father's elderly groom drove her away in the carriage. The girls stood motionless after their mother disappeared from sight until Miram, sensing their grief, gently wrapped her arms around them and held them close until they felt strong enough to run off into the garden.

As winter settled in, chill winds swept the valley, keeping the girls indoors. Miriam sensed their boredom and sometimes invited them to join her in the Oriental Room. This was her retreat – a corner of the house where she could be alone to write poetry or letters. Heavy crimson wallpaper lent an air of mystery to the room, an ideal backdrop for a profusion of her father's paintings that hung one above another on every wall.

When she brought Armgard and Sisi to this room, Miriam sat them on Egyptian cushions while she recited stories about her own childhood, describing travels with her father, the orientalist painter Wilhelm Gentz. Using his paintings as illustrations, she coloured their imagination with stories of caravan trips through the desert, the smell of spices in the markets of Smyrna and the

Miriam von Lambrecht-Benda

life of sultans at a time when the Ottoman Empire was still a potpourri of nationalities and religions.

Once spring broke through the leafless landscape, their mother began to spend less and less time in the sanatorium. But by then the girls had learnt to run to Miriam when they hurt themselves or had important news to share. They still sat with their grandmother in the afternoons under the old linden tree while she read stories she had written for them. Armgard snuggled close, taking in every word, while Sisi, always on her toes, eager to please, picked little blue flowers for her grandmother. '*Vergissmeinnichten*, the flowers of remembrance', Miriam murmured, adding that she hoped Sisi would always remember Stötterlinenburg and her German family, and one day bring her children to visit the house. As soon as she finished reading to Armgard, Miriam carried the forget-me-nots to her Oriental Room, where she placed them in a vase on her desk.

Sometimes Miriam played 'Grandmothers' Footsteps' with the girls and hugged them when they reached her; but when she called for bedtime nobody dared to argue.

One by one, as the years passed, the gardeners and then the butler left to fight the war. As the load on the housekeeper became more onerous, she brought her young son to help carry linen and sweep the floors. Hans, an only child, was six years older than Armgard; it was not long before the girls adopted him as their friend. From time to time Armgard and Sisi were allowed to eat their lunch in the kitchen with Hans and his mother – and then afterwards, while the housekeeper ironed sheets and tablecloths, he would take them to the stables, where he constructed a sit-on cart for them from the wheels of an old pram. In the early evenings, when he had finished helping his mother, he pulled them across the grass on the cart, causing uproarious laughter – especially when they fell off.

Despite the lack of help in the house, the von Lambrecht-Bendas still occasionally entertained small groups at the weekend. Their grandfather always seemed more cheerful when guests came to stay. Considerably older than his wife, he lacked her energy and enthusiasms. Before the war he had been in the habit of spending the coldest part of each winter in Monte Carlo, where he indulged his passion for gambling. Now even that pleasure was denied him. When there were no guests to entertain him, he enclosed himself in his study each morning, reading and rereading every newspaper he could find, even though he knew that censors had cut the unpalatable truth from every account of the battlefront. As the years passed, his best farm workers were recruited into the army, leaving only a bevy of women to bring in the harvest and stamp on the beet. He no longer invited Armgard and Sisi for trips in his pony trap. Among the friends who were invited to an occasional hunting weekend at Stötterlingenburg was Ambassador Solf, previously Germany's Minister for Foreign Affairs and later a staunch opponent of Hitler; his daughter, Lagi Solf, would one day play an important role in Armgard's life. Another weekend guest was Freiherr von Richthofen, a relative of the Red Baron, who was already known for his exploits as a fighter pilot. The girls liked these kindly men, yet could not understand how such people could find pleasure in hunting animals. Even Miriam, all-powerful in her own home, seemed to condone the killing. One day the girls crept into the larder while the guests were staying, hoping to find a tasty morsel to eat. They saw instead a table covered from one end to the other with the limp corpses of pheasants, hares, and even deer. Sisi had nightmares forever afterwards in which she saw their glazed eyes reproaching her – and trickles of blood dripping off the table to lie in puddles on the flagstone floor.

The guests they liked most of all were the young officers who came to Stötterlingenburg to spend part of their leave from the front. For some reason that Armgard and Sisi could not understand, these guests became quiet and withdrawn whenever they were questioned about their experiences on the battlefield. They gave monosyllabic answers to their hosts and never talked about bravery or comradeship, as was expected of them. The only enthusiasm they showed was for the food, asking for second helpings of beef, which their host carved for them, and home-made *flammerie*, made with stewed apples from the garden. Armgard and Sisi also ate with relish because, for the benefit of the officers, Miriam provided vastly superior food to the usual meagre fare at Stötterlingenburg during those long years of war.

The officers spent much of the day going for walks through the parklands alone, or sitting in the salon staring out of the window. Yet when Armgard and Sisi lured them into the garden to play, they behaved differently, laughing with a long warm chuckle at Sisi's jokes and telling Armgard how clever she was. Armgard could beat anyone at memory games – even the officers, no matter how many times they tried. When the men left to rejoin their regiment, the house echoed as though it were empty and the girls wandered listlessly from room to room, hoping to discover that one of the officers might somehow have been tempted to stay behind with the family to enjoy more of their grandmother's *flammerie*.

Now that Omi was permanently home at Stötterlingenburg, she sometimes talked to the girls about their father. She told them he had left Paris and was now working at the Norwegian Legation in London. Only until the end of the war, she assured them. Then they would all be together again.

Armgard wondered if he was an enemy, since he lived first

The von Lambrecht-Benda family with German Officers during the war. Standing l-r: Kurt, Feechen, Trudchen, Tante Sigrid, Sisi. Sitting: l-r: Omi, Miriam, and Armgard standing on step

in France and now in England, but their mother explained that Norway had remained neutral, so Norwegians were friendly to both sides. However Sisi, who had by now spent what seemed like most of her life away from her father, showed no interest at all in such a distant person. Besides, she and Armgard had a more pressing concern – Hans. Although he was still only fifteen, the housekeeper's son had been enlisted into the army. Miriam was angry about this, they could tell. Yet, although everyone normally did as she asked, the recruitment officer who came to the village seemed impervious to Miram's instructions that he should leave the boy at Stötterlingenburg, where his mother needed him. After Hans's departure the housekeeper sniffled into her handkerchief

Tante Sigrid with Sisi

all day long. Her husband had died a few months previously – bravely, they told her, from an enemy bullet. Her son was all she had.

One morning in November 1918, Armgard and Sisi decided to wander through the woodland that bordered the estate. Despite a bitingly cold wind, they preferred to be outdoors – anything to escape the air of gloom that pervaded the house. After a while they came to a road where an unusual rumbling caught their attention. Not far from where they stood a group of curious village women were staring in the direction of that noise. Soon it became clear that they were listening to the thud of approaching footsteps. A bedraggled line of soldiers gradually appeared in the distance.

The women gasped at their appearance. Hundreds shuffled along the road. They made no sound other than an eerie scrunch of boots on gravel. The men wore military uniform, yet they bore no resemblance to the serried rows of smart soldiers the girls had seen descending from the train onto the platform at the Belgium border just before the war. Many of the men tramping towards them were wrapped in bandages. Some, unable to walk unaided, hung on the shoulders of their comrades. The memory of those grey faces and staring eyes imprinted itself onto Armgard's mind like a sepia photograph, and remained there forever.

'They're on their way home', muttered one village woman to Armgard. 'God knows what will happen to us now.' But Armgard was concentrating on the faces of the soldiers, looking for Hans, even though some inner instinct already warned her that like his father he would never return.

The war had ended at last, but no sooner was the armistice signed than an influenza epidemic, so virulent in France that it had already killed thousands, was carried by returning troops and spread as quickly as a bushfire throughout Europe.

Even Stötterlingenburg was hit by the Spanish flu, as it soon became known. Miriam and Sisi somehow managed to retain their good health, while everyone around them fell victim to the fevers. Miriam as usual reigned supreme, nursing members of her own family and what little remained of her staff. Every family in the district had been affected, so there was no way she could obtain help. Most of the invalids pulled through, but Armgard showed no signs of improvement. The adults feared for her life as she lay stricken, her face a pale shade of blue. Often Miriam would appear in the middle of the night and lay herself on the bed close to Armgard, stroking her brow and giving her the strength to stay alive. Whenever he could make the time, the doctor drove to the house in the first private car anyone in the district had seen. When he entered Armgard's bedroom he would always find Sisi sitting on the windowsill nursing a limp doll on her lap. She pleaded with the doctor to help Armgard get better – and in time the miracle happened.

Once she was strong enough, Armgard came downstairs, where she was allowed to sit in her grandfather's chair by the fire while Sisi played quietly on the floor.

One day Omi showed them a telegram sent by their father from London. He had been posted back to the Foreign Office in Norway, and wrote to inform her that he would come straight from London to fetch her and the girls, and take them home to Oslo.

Armgard slumped back into the chair, begging her mother to let her stay at Stötterlingenburg with Miriam and Tante Sigrid. Sisi, seeing her mother's pained face, whispered to her sister that maybe it would be nice in Norway too. Their mother reassured them that they would not stay long in Norway, as Johan would soon be sent to a Legation in another country. Perhaps somewhere far from Europe. Sisi could tell that the idea of being far away from Europe appealed to her mother, and hoped Armgard would like that too.

But Armgard was inconsolable. As they lay in bed at night she told Sisi she planned to run away from Norway and come back to live with Miriam. Sisi offered to join her, yet part of her was afraid of the consequences. Torn in all directions, she felt almost as unhappy as her sister.

Meanwhile their mother was busy. First she made herself a new blouse from a piece of silk fabric that Miriam had saved for a special day, tucked away in her bottom drawer. Omi spent many hours with needle and thread before trying on the blouse in front of a mirror to check that the bias allowed the folds to fall in the most flattering manner, and that the neckline was low enough to show off her neck but not so low as to be deemed unsuitable in Johan's somewhat old-fashioned eyes. In the last days before her husband's arrival she made the journey into Osterwieck where, in 1908, she had bought gloves for her wedding. Many Huguenots had settled in the town and glove making was their contribution. Now, in the days leading up to Christmas 1918, the glove shop had closed its doors, and instead of Christmas decorations, clouds of defeat hung over every part of the village. Luckily Omi discovered that in a small street beside the Gothic church, the hairdresser was still doing her best to lift the ladies' spirits. She greeted Omi fondly and created an alluring coiffure that everyone at Stötterlingenburg admired. Sisi danced around her mother and, as the day drew closer, began to feel a glow of excitement about what lay ahead. But Armgard remained sullen. Even Tante Sigrid had difficulty making her laugh.

Although the war was over, their grandfather was also sullen. He barked at them if they made too much noise and hardly ever left his study. At meals he never mentioned his son-in-law – or Norway.

When the girls were called in from the garden one day to meet their father, moments after he stepped out of the carriage, Armgard barely recognised him and Sisi found nothing to love in this tall man who spoke a language she could no longer understand. Johan tried to win her round by speaking German, but her cheeks reddened with embarrassment as she listened to his funny accent. With studied politeness, Johan Michelet explained to Omi's parents that he had been unable to practice their language during these last four and a half years.

He stayed at Stötterlingenburg overnight, the briefest time possible, and in the morning the Michelet family set off in a carriage towards the station. Miriam and Kurt von Lambrecht-Benda made their farewells on the porch, standing beside the huge carved front doors that had long been a talking point among the neighbours up and down the country. The doors had been carved before the war by young craftsmen sponsored by Miriam. An amateur wood-carver herself, she had offered the young men accommodation in one of the flats above the stables and helped them secure commissions from her friends and acquaintances. In return for her sponsorship, they made the doors for her. 'These doors', she would tell her grand-daughters as they ran their hands across the smooth carvings, 'will still be standing long after I am gone. They will even be here when your grandchildren come to visit Stötterlingenburg'.

How fortuitous that as Miriam waved farewell to her daughter's family she remained ignorant of the cruel fate that would befall Stötterlingenburg in less than thirty years.

By the time the Michelet family reached the docks in Hamburg, from where they would embark on a trip across the wintry North Sea to Oslo, Omi and her daughters were tired and dishevelled. Johan, however, had kept his composure and strode in front of them, carrying his height proudly, using it as a prop to reinforce his authority. Before long he had reserved the best cabins and caught the eye of one of the few porters available, who agreed to carry their suitcases on board. As the ship steamed out of German waters towards his homeland, the family sat down together for a meal. By then the wind had whipped the sea into white anger, tipping the boat from side to side, causing both Omi and Sisi to lose their appetite. Johan ate heartily while he explained to his wife that although Norway remained neutral during the war, they were a seafaring nation who used their ships to transport food and ammunition to France and Britain. The Germans, he told her, sank many of those ships, with a heavy loss of life. Norwegians held their seamen in high esteem.

In Oslo the family rented a small apartment until such time as Johan was offered a posting abroad. Omi tentatively reached out to the friends she had made eight years previously when they lived for two years in Norway at the time of Sisi's birth. The young Norwegian mothers remembered her; they had been impressed and flattered by her effort to learn Norwegian. Now she was back amongst them, they invited her to their homes with Armgard and Sisi.

But at the formal dinner parties she and Johan attended, the atmosphere was daunting. Omi knew her accent gave her away immediately as a German. Unfortunately many of the men she met at these dinners could not forgive Germany for starting the war in Europe – nor for sinking their ships. The ties between Norway and Britain had always been strong and now the link had become more heartfelt than ever. Sometimes Omi sat at the dinner table looking politely from one gentleman to another but adding nothing to the conversation. Yet after a while it seemed that even her silence offended them. Johan showed sympathy and did his best to console her. He suggested she tell those men that she was now a Norwegian citizen and no longer German. After all, she had a Norwegian husband, a Norwegian passport and would soon be representing Norway in a foreign country. But Omi, having seen with her own eyes the devastation wrought by the humiliation of defeat, was incapable of abandoning ties to her own country and felt even more German than ever. Though she still wanted to win back the love of her husband, and realised this issue would always be a stumbling block between them, she found that the disdain many Norwegians showed towards Germany only strengthened the loyalty she felt for her homeland.

As soon as he received news that he had been appointed to serve as Minister at the first-ever Norwegian Legation to China, Johan hired a governess to ensure that his two daughters would continue speaking his language during the three long months of the journey – and for the duration of their stay in Peking. Unable to exert influence over his wife, he determined that his daughters' education and upbringing would turn them into loyal citizens of Norway.

3

Peking 1920-28

From the very beginning, Armgard told me, they hated the governess. She forced Norwegian on them while they were living in China, so naturally they were happier when neither the governess nor their father was around, because then they could speak German together. Mealtimes were also a problem. Only Norwegian was allowed, and the girls were expected to remain silent until an adult spoke to them. Sometimes whole meals were spent in silence. It is probable that their father felt frustrated hearing his daughters chattering non-stop to each other in German during the daytime. Or maybe he was frustrated because he never had the son he wanted – or because his marriage was falling apart. Armgard felt that in some way he took it all out on her, because she was the eldest.

My mother also used to tell me stories about life in Peking in the twenties, and these were corroborated by everything Armgard recounted. I could find no hint of any discord between the sisters. Quite the contrary. But whereas Armgard spoke openly about her parents' marital struggle, in my mother's stories no emotions were mentioned.

When they first arrived in China, the Michelet family – and of course the governess – moved into the Grand Hotel de Pékin (now the Beijing Hotel). From their windows they looked down over the glistening golden roofs of the Forbidden City.

It was not long before a house on Shi-Jia Hutong became available to them. It had once been a Manchurian palace and more recently the Danish Legation. The hutong, or lane, a dirt pathway no more than fifteen feet wide, was bordered with walled compounds, each of them entered through large lacquered doors. The girls ran off to explore their new home. Inside the compound were many buildings linked by covered walkways. They stared in awe at the generous-sized reception rooms of the Residence where they would be living. Then they ran across the garden to the stables, where they found grooms brushing the coats of horses or polishing carriages, and on the way back they peered into the meagre dwellings of the servants, a series of lean-to sheds against the boundary wall. Fortunately the Danish diplomats who lived there previously had installed glass windows when they turned the palace into a legation – though not everywhere. The servants still survived the icy winters with only paper pulled across their window frames.

The gaiety of the roaring twenties was celebrated even in Peking. The *dipsis* – as diplomats were known – led a comfortable life. The five great powers (France, Britain, the United States, Russia and Japan) had their own small kingdom behind large walls. Known as the Legation Compound, it consisted of many bungalows, a grand house for each of the Ministers and houses and barracks for the military. The *dipsis* obeyed their own laws and oversaw their own armies. Their free time was divided between the racecourse, where many owned racing ponies, the horseback paper-hunts out of town, the British Club and parties. Minor Legations, such as the Norwegian, were less ostentatious and had no army to protect them. Only one or two soldiers, recruited from General Munthe's elite Guards Battalion, stood on duty outside the Michelets' home.

When Omi discovered that the governess had fallen in love with a Swedish businessman she met on board ship during their long journey to China, and wanted to leave the Michelet household to marry him, she was secretly as overjoyed as her daughters. Since there were no Norwegian schools or even governesses in Peking, the girls were sent to the American Convent School. They were ten and twelve years old. English was a language quite new to them, but in time they found themselves at home amongst the other girls of mixed nationalities; Sisi had a natural talent for languages, while Armgard was thirsty for knowledge in whatever language she could find it. For the first time in her life Sisi was introduced to sport; she excelled at tennis and was soon invited to play in minor tournaments at the school.

But all was not well within the Michelet family. Johan no longer held his wife's hand in his nor kissed her cheeks as he left the house, and the girls struggled to win their father's favour. Like all who seek to please, Sisi ran to do his bidding and always spoke Norwegian in his presence, yet his demeanour remained dour. Armgard, on the other hand, kept out of his way whenever possible, pretending she no longer cared. During the long meals punctuated with periods of silence, she expressed her feelings by eating less and less until she became anorexic. It gave her a sense of control over her own body and even over her parents. They warned her she would die unless she ate properly but the more they cajoled and demanded, the less she ate.

Fortunately Johan and Omi were often at diplomatic functions in the evenings, so Armgard could eat a small amount of food with Sisi before disappearing to her room, where she read books in English or German until she fell asleep. Sisi, who preferred people to books, ran across the garden after dinner to the *amah's* room, where she was always made welcome. She loved watching the amah's long, plump silkworms spin cocoons over teacups or star-shaped pastry cutters. Sometimes the amah dipped the resulting silk into coloured water and gave it to Sisi as a bookmark to take to Armgard. On other occasions when she arrived in the amah's room an aroma of Chinese pancakes wafted through the window. Outside in the tiny courtyard, under an array of hanging birdcages, a greyish mixture of flour and water was cooking on a charcoal stove. The amah and Sisi would share the pancake when

Armgard and Sisi with Chinese friends

it emerged polka-dotted in black where it had burnt over the holes. It tasted delicious.

The girls always looked forward to the summer holidays. In order to escape the heat of a Peking summer, Omi rented a house with a tennis court each year at Peitaho (now Beidaihe), a beach resort three hundred kilometres south-east of Peking, blessed with warm sunshine and aquamarine-coloured sea.

Number One Boy, the most important member of their household, would arrange all the details of the move. Leaving a day in advance, he took some of the servants, including Number

One Cook and the Laundry Man, and all the necessary linen, china, glass, silver, wines, kitchen utensils, cushions for the verandah chairs, umbrellas for the beach, bridge table and cards, and suitcases full of summer clothes. Johan only made a couple of short visits to Peitaho during their three-month stay. He preferred to stay in Peking, where he rode his horses, hunted and attended the race meetings in town. As a result, Armgard loved the freedom of life at Peitaho, where she could once more talk German at any time of the day with Sisi and her mother.

Not only summer brought excitement for the girls. When the cold, dry air blew south from Siberia and the temperature in Peking reached well below zero, Omi organised huge picnics on the frozen canal. Six to eight people climbed onto each sledge, which was pulled along the ice by a series of coolies. The guests huddled under hot water bottles and fur rugs. From time to time the coolies stopped to let Armgard, Sisi and their friends clamber onto the ice so they could skate alongside the sledges. The cavalcade always ended at a temple outbuilding where Number One Boy had organised lunch. Seated at tables covered with white linen cloths and surrounded by charcoal fires to keep them warm, the guests enjoyed a three-course meal. Number One Boy had borrowed extra china and glass from some of the Michelets' friends. This was common practice in Peking, and Omi had long since ceased to be surprised when she ate off her own plates in someone else's house – or drank from friends' glasses at her own parties. As far as she could remember, nothing was ever broken or went missing.

During the spring of 1923, Omi and her daughters were invited to take tea with the Emperor and his wife in the Forbidden City. By then Emperor P'u Yi was seventeen years old. He had been anointed Lord of Ten Thousand Years when he was three, but two years later the government stripped him of power, ending the Ming dynasty. Instead of exiling the boy, they allowed him royal privileges providing he never left the Forbidden City. Though merely a puppet of government, he still presided over more than a hundred eunuchs. A Scottish tutor, Reginald Johnson, taught the Emperor to speak English and also modernised Palace life, building a tennis court and bringing in bicycles. In 1987 Bertolucci made a stirring film about P'u Yi, called *The Last Emperor*.

On the day they arrived to take tea at the palace, Omi, Armgard and Sisi were ushered by servants all the way from the huge gates on Tiananmen Square into the presence of P'u Yi and his young wife. She liked to call herself Empress Elizabeth because, thanks to Reginald Johnson, English names were fashionable among high-ranking ladies. She wore robes of heavy silk and poured tea for the Michelets with her slender oriental hands. Sisi was fascinated by her fingernails, carefully grown to a length of two inches and protected by shields of gold encrusted with jewels. These finger nails signified that she had no need to use her hands; instead she had a bevy of helpers to dress her, and scribes to write her letters. While Armgard and Sisi sat demurely in such exalted company, Omi conversed with the Emperor. Tall and slender, wearing horn-rimmed spectacles, he showed great interest in Europe, despite his tender years.

No sooner had the girls made themselves completely at home in the international atmosphere of Peking than a new challenge faced them. Their father insisted they leave the American school, where both were happy and successful, to spend two years at a Norwegian boarding school. While Sisi wept in front of her father, Armgard remained icily silent. Omi, powerless to help, could only distance herself still further from her husband, staying home with the girls whenever possible.

Perhaps if she had also borne him sons, she could have influenced at least her daughters' place of education. Perhaps if she were wealthy, she could have stood on firmer ground. However, the inheritance she had received after her father's death in 1922 never reached her. Her brother, in charge of remitting the money to an account in Peking, had allowed it to remain too long in a German bank at the very moment in history when Germany was suffering a crisis of hyperinflation. This turned out to be so serious that state banks printed paper money, devaluing the currency so that some people carried their salaries home in wheelbarrows and then rushed to spend it before its value dropped even lower. By the time Omi's inheritance reached China, the cost of the bank fees amounted to more than the money she received. She was left to rely, as she always had, on handouts from her husband.

Johan was due for home leave, paid for by the Norwegian government; he booked berths for the whole family on a P&O ship from Shanghai to Europe. After a brief holiday with his relations in Oslo, he formally escorted his daughters to their new school at Lillehammer.

Although Sisi suffered from homesickness during the first weeks of term, she gradually adapted to boarding-school life and made a few good friends among the Norwegian girls, one of whom remained close to her for the rest of their lives. However, Armgard was inconsolable from the first day. Having travelled widely herself, she found her fellow pupils parochial and the teachers were, in her opinion, no better. While others chattered and giggled in the evenings, she studied diligently, memorising details of Norwegian history and completing her homework in mathematics or religious studies. English language posed no problems for her, allowing her more time to get to grips with new subjects. By the end of the year she succeeded in passing every exam with honour and felt herself to be in a strong enough position to issue an ultimatum to her father. Telling him that if she were forced to stay at the school for another year she would become seriously ill, she proposed that she and Sisi should spend the summer holidays at Stötterlingenburg with Miriam, as planned, and then make their way back to Peking on their own.

Perhaps Johan was persuaded by her letter, or maybe he received the same message from the school or from his brother in Oslo, because he did agree to the plan.

At Stötterlingenburg, despite the absence of their grandfather, who had died two years previously, the girls found little had changed. The person who mattered most to them, Miriam, still reigned supreme; she once more took them under her wing, introducing them to her latest artistic protégés and guiding them through her prolific new vegetable garden. Making their stay yet more memorable was Tante Sigrid, who joined them for the entire holidays with her three young sons. Armgard and Sisi felt at home once more and enjoyed the privilege of being the older cousins this time, playing games with the boys and reading them stories before they went to bed at night. They even took their enthusiastic young cousins on adventurous trips into the woods to look for mushrooms, just as Tante Sigrid used to do with them during the war.

In August 1925, Armgard and Sisi bid farewell to Miriam and travelled to Stockholm, from where they started their long journey to Peking. Their uncle had discovered that a Norwegian couple would also be travelling on the Trans Siberian Railway in September so, although none of the family knew these people, it was arranged that they should meet Armgard and Sisi in Stockholm and travel to China with them. The girls were fifteen and fourteen years old.

On their way to Moscow to start their train journey, they stopped for a day in Petrograd (later Leningrad and now St Petersburg) where, together with the Norwegian couple, they strolled along the banks of the Neva. A Russian couple with a dignified appearance stood watching the four sightseers as they approached. Dressed in what must once have been elegant clothes but were now nothing more than well-darned patchworks of good fabric, the Russians remained stationary in front of them as though they longed to beg, yet could not bring themselves to stoop so low. Without a word spoken, they created for Armgard an image of life in post-revolutionary Russia that she never forgot.

Other images of the Russian tragedy were to be seen all around them. In Moscow the girls stayed with the father of one of their school friends, Herr Urby, at the Norwegian Legation. The Legation was housed in what had been, until the revolution, the home of a Russian aristocrat. Once master of his own house, the aristocrat and any number of his relatives now occupied the basement. Herr Urby took the young visitors downstairs to meet these once-influential Russians and, as she walked in to the main living room, Armgard tripped over the edge of the carpet. Rising to her feet, she noticed the reason for her fall: the family had piled their valuable Persian carpets one on top of another in the only space they had.

Around the room were stacked a profusion of large pieces of fin-de-siècle furniture and paintings – as much as the family could cram in from their previous existence. And yet, the girls were told, these aristocrats considered themselves fortunate to have the Norwegians – rather than Bolsheviks – occupying their home and the freedom to live as they chose in their own basement.

Other than the Norwegian Legation, the only luxury Armgard and Sisi encountered in Russia was the Orient Express, which they boarded in Moscow and which would be their home for the next ten days. Since the railway lines were much wider than in Europe, the compartments were spacious. With one bed used as a sofa during the day, and another folded away above the window, it felt more like a sitting room than a sleeper. Only the sheets on their beds were a reminder of the collapse of Russia's economy since the revolution. Instead of fine linen, they were made of paper.

Once on the train, Armgard took charge of both their passports. She had been warned that if she lost them, she and Sisi would never get out of Russia. She wore the passports in a hand-made bag that hung round her neck during the daytime and lay under her pillow at night. The two girls passed their days watching the never-ending forests of birch trees through the windows and doing crossword puzzles; when they had finished every puzzle in the book, they invented more for each other. This must have been an incongruous battle of wits, as both girls had appalling spelling in every language.

The train stopped each day for refuelling with coal, or sometimes wood. During those stops Armgard and Sisi would climb down on to the platform to buy tea, honey, butter, cheese and fruit and make a picnic in the compartment of the Norwegian couple.

They also stopped at Yekaterinburg, a name that will be forever associated with a brutal murder. It was here, six years earlier, that Tsar Nicholas and all his family were killed. Some of the passengers on the train with Armgard and Sisi were Russian aristocrats fleeing from those same Bolsheviks. As they approached the station the girls saw the huge fort that loomed over the platform as if to remind them of the power the Bolsheviks still retained. The atmosphere on board grew tense. Nevertheless, all passengers were asked to come onto the platform, where a simple supper had been laid out at one long table. Armgard sat opposite a Russian soldier who had come to join them from the fort. She watched while he slowly cleaned his fingernails, one by one, with the pointed ends of his fork; otherwise he was dirty all over. Once back on the train, a discreet sigh of relief could be heard as the train started on its journey once more.

When they neared the border between Russia and China some of the passengers, discovering that Armgard and Sisi possessed diplomatic passports, brought along their cameras, begging the girls to carry them through customs. Armgard packed some of these cameras in their suitcases and hung others round their necks. Sure enough, theirs was the only luggage not searched and robbed; none of the Chinese customs officials questioned the diplomats' daughters' need for two or three cameras each.

While many of the Russian passengers stayed on in Harbin, in northern China, hoping that in time they would be able to earn enough money to make their way further south, Armgard and Sisi boarded another train for Peking, arriving on 24th September 1925, Armgard's sixteenth birthday.

They soon discovered that during their absence from China, serious changes had taken place. The young Emperor no longer lived in the Forbidden City and warlords were fighting to gain control of the city. For many months the residents of Peking had been suffering. Looting was widespread and when a thief was caught, he was decapitated on the spot and his head left in a box at the main gates to deter others. Because the city was surrounded, food and fuel became increasingly scarce. Even diplomats suffered. Throughout that long winter the Michelet family wore winter coats indoors in an attempt to keep warm. It was not until Chang

Johan in his first car

Tso-lin took over the reins of power that some sort of normality returned.

In time life became enjoyable again. Johan ordered the first car he had ever owned. It was specially designed with a hood high enough to accommodate not only his above average height, but also his top hat which he liked to wear whilst being driven through the city.

Omi and Johan had begun to give dinner parties once more for a wide group of friends, including the Italian writer, Daniel Varé, General Munthe and the novelist Ann Bridge, whose book *Peking Picnic* had as its centrepiece a Legation, describing parts of the Michelets' house and garden in great detail. The girls enjoyed meeting their parents' guests: now they were older they were sometimes allowed to join the adults for dinner. Another well-known person who visited the Michelets on several occasions was

Wallis Spencer, later the Duchess of Windsor. She lived at the time in Shanghai with her first husband, sometimes travelling north to Peking to stay with their friends the Rogers, who lived near the Norwegian Legation.

Omi also befriended many aristocratic Russian immigrants, who still flooded into China. They arrived with little money and no work experience. Sympathising with their plight, she employed one of them, *Melle* (short for Mademoiselle), to be the girls' governess and to tutor them in French and a little Russian. Melle joined in their fun and, best of all, she brought her friends to stay at the Michelet villa in Peitaho.

By now Armgard was eighteen years old. She showed off her slim figure and dark auburn hair with eye-catching fashions. Young men were eager to escort her to parties, but her ambition lay elsewhere. She excelled at school and the American nuns offered to arrange a place for her at a university in the United States. Longing to immerse herself in literature and history, she dreamt of graduating with top honours, which would lead her to a career as a journalist or a writer. Her English was already good enough to cope with any assignment she might be given, though she knew there was room for improvement. She hugged her dreams to herself for a day or two, before finding the courage to confront her father.

She expected difficulties, but was not prepared for the unequivocal dismissal of everything she hoped for. Her father told her there was no reason for her to attend university. She was destined to find a husband and in his opinion the learning would simply be wasted. In the meantime she could be useful at his side; a daughter – especially one as attractive as Armgard – was always an asset to a head of mission. He would not pay for her to attend university in America.

Armgard kept her wretchedness wrapped up and hidden, spending hours with a book in her room. Omi offered comfort in her own way, but gave Armgard the impression that secretly she agreed with her husband that university would be a waste of Armgard's time. Sisi did her best to help, organising outings with their Chinese friends to distract her sister. On the surface it appeared that Armgard was getting over her disappointment, but deep inside she felt a fermenting resentment against her father. She wanted to take charge of her own life and fulfil her potential, yet she was powerless in his hands.

Meanwhile diplomatic life went on as usual. In January 1928 a messenger arrived at the Legation, inviting the Norwegian Minister, his wife and their daughters to dinner with Chang Tso-lin. By then the warlord had installed himself in the Forbidden City, taking young white Russians as his concubines

The Michelets drove once more to the entrance in Tiananmen Square, where they were met by lantern-carrying servants, who guided them up the marble stairs, past lotus ponds to a small pavilion with frescoes painted on the outside. On the steps they were met by an interpreter and two of Chang Tso-lin's adjutants.

Chang, small and dark, was said to have started off as a bandit before conquering the northern provinces, yet he behaved with grace and courtesy, welcoming them at the doorway of his pavilion. They sat at a table for eight: Chang, two interpreters, a bodyguard and the four Michelets. Chang Tso-lin was talkative, having a good knowledge of foreign politics. Silently gliding servants placed dish after dish of extravagant Chinese food on the table. There were bear paws, a rare delicacy, followed by Peking duck, shark fins and swallows' nests with very old black eggs that had been buried in the soil. Chang used his own chopsticks to serve his guests; this was considered a great honour.

Six months later, to their great distress, the Michelets learnt that Chang Tso-lin had been killed. By now Chiang Kai-shek had gained leadership of the Kuomintang and was approaching Peking from the south. Chang Tso-lin fled from the Forbidden City and attempted an escape back to Mukden (now Shenyang) in Manchuria. But the train in which he was travelling was blown up by the Japanese Army. What little remained of him, his Russian concubines and the works of art he took with him from the Forbidden City, were strewn far across the barren landscape.

But by then the Michelet family had started preparing their departure from China and attended a series of farewell parties in their honour. The Norwegian Foreign Office had appointed Johan to be Minister at the Legation in Rio de Janeiro.

Sisi could barely contain her excitement. She loved warm weather and the romance of balmy evenings. In her mind's eye she was already strolling along Copacabana beach, a full moon overhead and a handsome man beside her. Who would he be? A diplomat, perhaps. Diplomatic life appealed to her. She had recently started imitating Armgard's mannerisms and style of dress in the hope that once they had settled in Rio some man might find her almost as attractive as her sister.

On the boat to Europe. Omi, centre, with Armgard and their friend Frau Johanna (Hanna) Solf (later to become founder of the Solf Circle)

4

Rio de Janeiro 1928-34

Some years after my father's death, my younger brother, Tim, retrieved a diary from one of the many chests of documents our father had accumulated over the years. When he eventually read the diary, written in Brazil in the 1930s, Tim discovered - to his astonishment - that our father was once in love with Armgard. This had never been mentioned by either of our parents.

'Is it true that Daddy loved Armgard?' Tim and I badgered our mother. Perhaps it's cruel to rake up the past, but we felt we had a right to know.

She twisted her wedding ring round her finger while she attempted to compose some sort of answer to this inconvenient line of questioning. Brought up in a family that discussed facts rather than feelings, she had always tidied away the less desirable memories of the past and swept them from her mind. We waited quietly while she gathered her confused thoughts.

'My sister was always much prettier than me.' She hoped this would be enough to satisfy our thirst for the truth, but we carried on. Gently we pursued our same line of questioning until we finally had our answer.

'I don't think she loved him really. Not like I did. I loved Rio and I loved Paddy, yet my mother took me away from both. She took me to Germany. I was angry with her about that.'

I hugged my mother, realising how lucky I was to have had such an easy life compared to hers. Would I have felt unwilling to divulge stories if so many hurdles had been placed in my way? Was her adult repression of feelings bound up with her youth? Or did it only start when war broke out, turning the world as she knew it upside down? I was determined to find out.

My brothers and I had grown up hearing stories about the gaiety of Rio de Janeiro before the war, now we had my father's diaries to give detail to the pictures painted with such enthusiasm by my mother.

It was two years after the Michelet family arrived in Rio that the Royal Mail Lines ship SS *Almanzora* ambled her way down the Brazilian coastline, pulling alongside the quay first at Pernambuco, then at Bahia, to deliver and collect mail. After a stormy journey from Southampton in the south of England, she held steady on her last leg into Rio, leaving a reflection of herself on the sun-dappled water. Dolphins and flying fish cruised alongside, escorting the ship into harbour.

On Sunday 13th September 1931 Paddy Noble, a young British diplomat, stepped ashore. Nobody who sails into the bay of Rio de Janeiro for the first time is likely to forget the experience. Nothing, Paddy wrote in his diary, could ever diminish its beauty. It was not only Sugar Loaf Mountain that caught his eye, but also the line of hills that ran parallel to the town and in places seemed barely five hundred feet from the long, crescent-shaped beaches. There were five of them: Beirama, Flamengo, Botafogo, Copacabana and Ipanema.

He had been appointed First Secretary at the British Embassy. His Ambassador would be Sir William Seeds, a man known for his sharp and sometimes impatient mind; Paddy looked forward to working at his side and felt confident he would be able to achieve the high standards expected of him. During the two-and-a-half-week journey, he had devoted every morning to learning Portuguese. He had a talent for languages, having studied Latin and Greek before the age of ten and later, after university, spent six months in Europe, first in Berlin and later in Rome, while studying for the Foreign Office entrance exams. Portuguese was a new challenge and one he relished; though by no means fluent, he could already make sense of the Brazilian newspapers. This would be Paddy's first posting abroad. He was nearly twenty-seven years old.

Before embarking on this journey to Brazil, he had lived at his parents' London home, a large terraced house, 43 Portland Place, a once-fashionable street that runs from Regent's Park

Paddy in his first
diplomatic uniform

down to Oxford Circus. He drove himself to work each morning in an Armstrong Siddeley, which his father had given him for his twenty-first birthday. Habits set in during a person's formative years, and my father's preference for rising late began during his first years at the Foreign Office. He was expected at work at 11am every morning and then, as a new recruit to the diplomatic service, advised to stay on until all the work of the day was finished. Normally this would be around 6pm, but just occasionally he was still at his desk at midnight. He earned £200 a year, with an extra £98 cost-of-living allowance – not adequate for an extravagant lifestyle, but since he lived at home he was comfortable enough.

The depression that hit America on 29th October 1929, one

year after he joined the Diplomatic Service, would gradually affect Britain, where it was known as 'The Slump'. Only two countries suffered as deeply as America; they were Austria and Germany. In London most people felt the pinch in some manner or another, but life continued much as it always had. Being an eligible bachelor, Paddy was invited to a string of social events; if he went to a dinner party, where there were usually about twelve guests, he was expected to wear white tie and tails. When he and his sister Rosemary were invited first to the theatre and then afterwards to a dance, he wore not only white tie and tails, but also a pair of spotlessly clean white kid gloves. Sometimes he was invited to an informal dinner followed by a game of bridge. On these occasions the hostess would tell him, 'Don't dress up, just wear black tie'.

Yet he was equally happy to sit quietly at home in the evening and read. A considerable collection of books filled every available shelf in his room and he had the ability to remember the details of each and every one of them. They ranged from a history of Scotland to Agatha Christie's newest detective story or a compendium of sporting achievements. The books he read in preparation for his journey to Brazil were carefully packed in his trunk and he watched now as they were unloaded from the ship into an Embassy car.

From the window of his room in the Copacabana Hotel – one of the less expensive rooms, lacking a beach view – he looked out over a roofscape of Rio and contemplated the two years that stretched ahead of him. He would miss Rosemary most of all. Although he had another sister and two brothers, it was with Rosemary he had shared everything from the beginning. Fifteen months apart, they played together as children in Scotland, attended the same London balls, spent holidays with the same friends and, above all, supported each other in times of need.

Would he find a soul mate in Rio? And how would he cope with the diplomatic cocktail party circuit where everyone would already know each other and he would be a stranger in their midst? At least he was good at remembering names; that would stand him in good stead. He hoped to find some serious Brazilians who might share his love of history and literature. He had not yet learnt to make the small talk he knew was expected of diplomats serving abroad. But Rio, he soon discovered, had a charm of its own, which reached out to embrace newcomers, drawing them into its heart and imbuing them, often against their better judgement, with the gaiety of the city. Though there was little that might pass as culture in the European sense, Brazil's capital city was comfortable with its own hedonism. Europeans either despised it or loved it. Within weeks of his arrival, Paddy threw his British caution to the wind and made up his mind to love it.

But there was also work to be done at the Embassy – from 10am to 6pm. Sometimes the load grew strenuous; in 1932, eleven months after his arrival, the British Embassy found itself responsible for helping its own citizens trapped in São Paulo during a civil war. The local Paolista Revolutionary Party had risen up against its government in Rio and, on 9th July, five students who were asking for a change in the constitution were gunned down by troops. Their deaths so incensed the people of São Paolo that the Paolistas embedded themselves firmly and their armed revolt brought chaos to the city over many months. During the early part of that uprising Paddy and the archivist worked twelve-hour days organising channels of communications for British businesses, somehow managing to charter a banana boat to collect British passport holders from one of the ports near São Paulo and carry them to safety. He enjoyed the hard work, gaining confidence in his own abilities and the sense of doing something worthwhile for his country.

Only three countries merited embassies in Brazil in the 1920s: the United States, Britain and France. The rest were represented by Legations. The Norwegian Legation, at 92 Rua Alice, stood part-way up a tree-lined hill and looked down over the strip of town between itself and the beach. By the time Paddy arrived in

Lunch on Copacabana Beach. Armgard on left, Sisi on right

Rio, Armgard and Sisi Michelet were well settled into a Brazilian pace of life and had many friends; they were twenty-one and twenty years old.

The workload of their father, the Norwegian Minister, was seldom onerous, allowing him time to read French literature and ride his horses out into the countryside, preferably in the company of some charming women. Omi never rode. She could usually be found puffing on a cigarette at the bridge table, or hosting a party. Every evening at about six, she threw open the Legation doors to friends – and to the young people who formed part of Armgard and Sisi's circle. Surrounded by swaying palm trees, the house had a welcome modesty about it, yet was large enough for entertaining many people in an informal manner. Often guests would wander through onto the balcony, where they chatted amiably while the moon, red as the inside of a watermelon, rose into the sky.

It was Sisi who first invited Paddy to join a party of friends at the Norwegian Legation and soon he became a regular visitor. She would run over to welcome him and lead the way to the balcony where the young congregated. There she would lean against the balustrade, encouraging him to tell stories about his life in London.

Every time he was invited to a dance, he told her, it was necessary to wear a pair of clean white kid gloves, because the ladies would not have liked their dancing partners to dirty their elaborate dresses with bare hands or even smutty gloves. But Paddy soon found out it cost so much to get those gloves cleaned after each party that sometimes he didn't go to another ball all week.

Another frequent guest at the Norwegian Legation was Julie Hubrecht, daughter of the Dutch Minister. In her Memoirs, published in 1995, Julie wrote:

My very special friend in Rio was Armgard Michelet (also her sister Sisi)daughters of the Norwegian Minister. Armgard had lovely red hair, and my mother, deploring the fact that none of her children had red hair, painted her portrait.

Julie later married a wealthy Swedish businessman, Holger Graffman, who would become a pivotal agent for the Allies during the war. Julie and Armgard met again in Stockholm fourteen years later, under very different circumstances.

When Noel Coward made a visit to Rio he organised a treasure hunt for the young international crowd. As he was already famous on both sides of the Atlantic for his plays, *Hay Fever* and *Private Lives*, invitations to meet him were in great demand. Sisi invited Paddy to be her partner for the evening. The clues, which Coward wrote himself, were in verse. Each couple had to decipher the first clue, climb into their car and drive to wherever it indicated. There they would find the next verse waiting for them. And so it went on for two hours, followed by a dinner given in Noel Coward's honour. At about 1.30am the great man himself stood up and sang 'Some day I'll find you', 'I'll see you again' and 'Every little bird can fly'. Both Paddy and Julie Hubrecht would later confide in their respective memoirs how much they regretted not keeping Coward's hand-written ditties for the treasure hunt.

Whenever Paddy appeared at a party or diplomatic reception, Sisi spotted him out of the corner of her eye and, making excuses to her companions, moved inconspicuously towards him. He warmed to her friendly manner and always accepted her invitations. At her side he met many young Brazilians, as well as other foreigners like himself.

Yet time and again he found himself seeking the company of Armgard. She was without doubt the more beautiful of the two sisters but seemed unaware of the trump card she held. However, it would have been more than her auburn hair and good looks that attracted Paddy. They had much in common. Both were reserved and shared a love of reading. Both enjoyed discussing the merits of a film they had seen – or wider issues such as the nature of patriotism or the harm caused by the depression. Only six months after his arrival in Rio, on 4th May 1932, Paddy wrote in his diary:

After dinner went round to invite François to bridge tomorrow; he took me on to join Sisi and go to a movie; we went to Wächter's where Armgard was, and finally I left François and Sisi to go on to the movie and I stayed and talked for a bit and then I took Armgard home. I stayed for half an hour or so and failed to get away before Mme Michelet came in.

And three weeks later:

The dance was a magnificent success and it didn't end until 4am. According to Mme. Rubems de Mello I am supposed to be engaged to Armgard.

It was easy for young people to live and party in Rio. Seduced by music and moonlight and love and romance, they barely noticed the humidity that settled over them during the summer. Only if they ran their hand along the top of a car as they left a party

Armgard and Paddy
in Petrópolis

were they aware of the effects of the humid air; their hand would be so wet they could shake off the water. However, the British Ambassador, Sir William Seeds, found the humidity intolerable; in December he moved the entire Embassy up to Petrópolis, to escape the summer heat. The town, once the Imperial City of Brazil, stood high above Rio, one hour's drive up a winding road through lush tropical forests. The Ambassador took over a large villa, to which many of the Embassy files and records were taken. Paddy was instructed to stay nearby in a small hotel. However, instead of relishing the dry air of Petrópolis, he found that he was

Armgard in
Rio de Janeiro

missing his friends in Rio.

Luckily Armgard and Sisi knew plenty of young men willing to drive them up to Petrópolis at the weekend. While Sisi and her friends played tennis on a private court in one of the many rented villas, Armgard and Paddy wandered into the new cathedral, pretending to study its architecture.

By the end of January the British Embassy was once more settled in Rio – and partying with the young set began all over again for Paddy. He was also expected to attend formal dinner parties in the homes of senior Brazilian businessmen and politicians, and to support and befriend the British community. On 11th November 1932 he wrote in his diary:

In the morning went to Armistice Service. It was rather impressive in that small unostentatious church, a little bit of England far away from home. The service was dignified and somehow friendly, though they produced a ridiculous tinkly tune for 'Valiant Hearts' and the organist forgot the last verse of 'For All the Saints'. I couldn't help thinking of the madness of the last war, the wanton destruction of young men, boys of 19 and less, and the futile pigheaded diehards who say that war is inevitable and don't realise the shame of such an admission.

While he was living in Berlin – to improve his German before he sat the Foreign Office exam – Paddy would have listened to muted accounts of the war from a German perspective. Here in Brazil he heard them in more detail from Armgard, as she recounted stories about the humiliation of defeat suffered by her family at Stötterlingenburg.

'Patriotism, nationalism, call it what you like, can be so harmful', Armgard told me many years later. 'Paddy understood what I was saying. We used to discuss how any strong leader can whip up patriotism to their own advantage for the purpose of sport or propaganda or – eventually – war. It's no good for anything else; it just narrows people's minds and encourages them to look down on or even dislike those from a different background. Paddy was never like that', she told me. 'He found out what people were worth, not where they came from.'

After eight months Paddy and Armgard were inseparable:

After the concert we went to the Kammerers for a reception and danced a bit. I didn't stay long and took Armgard home, not quite direct.

By now Harriet Michelet, Armgard and Sisi's Norwegian cousin, had arrived to join them in Rio. Although at nineteen she was a year younger than Sisi, the two girls shared a sense of fun and dedicated themselves to making the most of Rio's heady way of life. Harriet's presence made it easier for Sisi to ignore the blossoming romance between Paddy and Armgard, or pretend it did not concern her. Johan showed his pleasure at the growing friendship between Harriet and Sisi, nodding in approval when he heard them chattering together in Norwegian.

Rio at that time had a population of a little over a million inhabitants. As Paddy discovered during his working day at the Embassy, Brazilians were a happy-go-lucky people. Even among top politicians, whose co-operation he needed, there existed an unspoken agreement that it would be just as good to get things done tomorrow as today – and the day after would be even better. A football match or Carnival held more importance for most Brazilians than the dull realities of life, such as foreign affairs or economics. And so Paddy, once used to a disciplined work ethic, learnt to accept the Brazilian way of life, no longer expecting an immediate response from his Brazilian counterparts, learning instead to control the impatience he might once have felt and to sit back in an almost Brazilian fashion, contemplating the evening ahead.

Every year, just before the beginning of Lent, Carnival drew virtually the whole population of Rio into its thrall. Harriet Michelet remembered Carnival in 1933 as one of the highlights of her life. From Saturday midday until Wednesday at the same time, everything shut. Shops, banks and even government offices shut for the duration. It was a party for everyone – rich or poor, civil servants or road sweepers – they all joined in the fun. Together with Sisi and her friends, Harriet danced in the streets

Off to Carnival. l-r: Sisi, a friend, Armgard, a friend, Julie Hubrecht and Paddy

until dawn – night after night. Although they started the evening with their own friends, they soon joined in with the general throng of revellers. There were no social barriers during Carnival. Crime and sexual advances, as far as they could discover, did not exist – dancing and singing were enough to thrill the crowds. Sambas, tangos, rumbas, la bamba – it was the rhythm that kept them going. Harriet and Sisi danced with the waiter from the local restaurant, their wealthy Brazilian friends, the policeman on duty, the man who ran the corner shop – or complete strangers.

Paddy also remembered Carnival that year and wrote in his diary:

We had dinner at the Norwegian Legation then went down to the Avenida Rio Branco to watch the floats make their way through the crowds to thunderous applause from tens of thousands of spectators. After the floats had gone, the crowds, including us, swarmed into the streets and formed snakes, each one holding the waist of the person in front. So we moved from one dance place to another; I remember at one, it may have been the Jockey Club, I saw our Embassy legal advisor, normally rather a serious man, with a paper hat on his head, singing an absurd song that started: 'Monkey look at your tail'. Very much the spirit of Carnival. Naturally there was a tendency for the party to split up into couples, smiled on by a moon that rose red out of a rolling Atlantic.

Soon after this entry, Paddy's diary stopped and, as far as we know, he never wrote one again. This was 1933, and his romance was coming to an end. Was he so upset by Armgard's eventual rejection or was it pure coincidence that he had no time to write a diary? He often talked to us about the gaiety of Rio, the fun he had there, without ever suggesting a romance with anyone other than Sisi. Perhaps if certain consequences of Hitler's war had been different, he might have felt willing to tell us about that period of his life.

Sixty years later, Armgard explained her own point of view to me. 'Paddy and I had good times together. I never wanted to hurt him but in the end I did. I knew I wasn't suited to being a diplomat's wife. I wanted to live near my grandmother – where I had roots – and not be trailed around the world like a piece of hand-baggage. And I wanted a job – I yearned to become a journalist and use my brain – to be someone in my own right. You can't do those things when you're married to a diplomat and I had high hopes for myself.'

Ending her romance with Paddy was painful for both of them, she said, but she knew that the biggest challenge to her ambition for an independent life would be her father. He had always felt the need to be in charge of his family – to be consulted on all things. He made it quite plain to his daughters that, just as he enjoyed seeing them benefit from the foreign travel and social life his diplomatic office bestowed on them, he also expected them to be a compliment to him and an asset to his career.

But Armgard was now twenty-three years old and ambitious. As the daughter of a diplomat, however, she was not allowed to earn money in the country to which he was accredited. She was still totally dependent on her father.

Determined to break loose, and quite prepared to sacrifice the privileges and protection that her father's career brought her, she planned an escape. Waiting until he was in a good mood after a long ride across the countryside, she entered her father's study. Play-acting a confidence she did not feel, Armgard explained that she would like to return to Europe immediately, rather than wait a year until his tour of duty in Rio ended. She reminded him that Berlin was recovering from its financial depression and that, thanks to the new Chancellor, Herr Hitler, Germans had regained their confidence and were eager to succeed at every level. She explained that she would be able to live in Berlin with her aunt Sigrid and would therefore not be a burden on his pocket. She planned to take a secretarial course as the first step on the road towards a career in journalism.

Considering her request, Johan sat for a long time in silence. No doubt he even tried to put himself in her shoes for once because, albeit reluctantly, he agreed to let her go. Offering to pay a small stipend to enable her studies, he wished her well.

For the first time in her life, Armgard's future lay in her own hands.

After Armgard sailed out of Rio in the middle of 1933, Sisi and Harriet continued to enjoy themselves under the spell of Rio's charm. Most mornings the girls went to Copacabana beach, where they met a group of their friends. Sometimes Omi joined them. When he returned from dropping Johan at his office, the chauffeur would drive the three of them to the beach, pulling the car up onto the edge of the sand. Resplendent in a white summer uniform, he erected a tent further down the beach to shade the ladies and then retreated to wait by the car. Occasionally, on a Sunday, Johan announced his intention of joining the beach party. He stepped out of the car in his formal grey suit and shoes, carrying a cane with a silver top. Having never swum in his life, he preferred to stroll along the beach, appreciating the pretty women of all ages and occasionally stopping for a brief conversation with one of them.

When Harriet and Sisi were not at the beach, they took part in tennis tournaments at the club. Sisi, who had been a keen

Sisi (with flowers) and Harriet boarding the ship for Europe. Three friends came to bid them farewell

member of the tennis team at her American school in Peking, frequently came away with the winner's cup. Tumbling with ease in and out of Portuguese, German, Norwegian or English, Sisi made herself popular with both Brazilians and the international set. Gradually she began including Paddy in her circle again. They danced together at parties. She threw herself wholeheartedly into making sure everyone enjoyed themselves as much as she did. Without her, parties lacked a cornerstone; she led the dancing, she was the music of the dance. Paddy learnt new steps in her company and soon moved as she did, with an almost Latin rhythm. To his surprise he enjoyed dancing and came back willingly for more.

But Omi, watching over her younger daughter with tender concern, and bearing in mind the difficulties of her own marriage of mixed nationalities, made a sudden decision. Explaining to Johan that she could no longer cope with the humid weather, she announced to him that Sisi and Harriet would accompany her now to Germany, rather than wait until his tour of duty ended the following year. Harriet could then sail back to Norway from Hamburg, while Omi and Sisi took the train to Berlin. Reminding her husband that he seemed happier in the company of his various female riding companions than with her, Omi bought tickets for the journey. He had no choice but to acquiesce to her decision.

At the beginning of 1934, bitterly disappointed at having to leave, Sisi bid a sad farewell to the friends she had made in Brazil, to Rio itself, which she loved with all her heart, and to Paddy Noble, to whom she had given Tante Sigrid's address in Berlin.

She wondered if she would ever see him again.

5

Armgard's Wedding 1934

The First World War had left Armgard with a deep love of her grandmother and of the Harz Mountains. Now Berlin was working its magic on her. By September 1933, when she arrived in the city, it had become one of the most exciting capitals of Europe. Most Germans believed that Hitler was giving Germany back its standing in the world and improving the economy. Now they could enjoy world-class art and music, as well as theatre and an almost unparalleled night-life. The few who had qualms about the power the Nazi Party had acquired since coming to office tended to keep quiet about their fears.

Six months after Armgard's arrival, Sisi and her mother also came to stay in Tante Sigrid's house. The three young sons of the family, who already adored Armgard, were delighted that Sisi had arrived to join her sister. Bolko, the only one of Tante Sigrid's three boys to survive the war, remembered those weeks in 1934 when Armgard and Sisi stayed at their house in Berlin. He and his twin brother were twelve years old at the time, and so entranced with the girls that they followed them like puppies around the house. '*Always I admired my two cousins Armgard and Sisi*', he wrote to me, '*because they had painted their foot nails red when wearing sandals*'. The boys had never seen anything like it.

Soon Omi decided to rent an apartment for herself and her daughters, settling into Berlin life as comfortably as if it were a well-loved armchair. Not far from where they lived, Unter den Linden stretched for a mile from Brandenburg Gate towards the east. One of the most famous boulevards in the world, it was named after the rows of linden (lime) trees that shade pedestrians. On either side stood fashion houses, jewellery shops, grand hotels and the imposing facades of the Opera House and State Library. On Sundays, at twelve thirty in the afternoon, Omi liked to stop at the Ehrenmal Memorial, where trumpets paid homage to Germans who had died in the Great War. Each time she listened to those trumpets and read the words on the memorial, tears that she had no power to stop ran down her cheeks.

Armgard was also busy. She worked diligently at her typing course and in the evenings joined up with a congenial group of people. Although most of them were introduced to her after her arrival in Berlin, Lagi Solf was an old friend.

Lagi's father was the same Wilhelm Heinrich Solf, then

Foreign Minister, who had been a favourite of Armgard and Sisi at Stötterlingenburg during the First World War. He was currently serving as Germany's Ambassador to Japan. Although many of Armgard's friends were full of praise for the boost Hitler had given the German economy, Herr Solf vehemently opposed the Nazi regime from the start. After his death in 1936, his wife and daughter would start to collect like-minded people around them and become a focus for anti-Nazi intellectuals. In later history books their meetings became known as the *Solf-Kreis* or Solf Circle.

But in 1934, Lagi Solf, home from Japan, was still happy to party and enjoy herself. Her circle of friends was an eclectic group of Berliners; Armgard was thrilled to become a part of it – to belong.

One evening Lagi gave a party at which she introduced Armgard to Anton Knyphausen, a journalist working for the influential *Deutsche Allgemeine Zeitung*.

From the moment he entered the room, Armgard watched the ease with which Anton moved among the guests, displaying every appearance of complete self-confidence. She soon learnt that although he had solid roots in German high society, he also had a wide circle of artistic friends. Women found him attractive, often walking across the room to speak to him, yet, although he was cultured and well read, Armgard was surprised to find how little he had travelled. As the two of them became acquainted with one another he explained that during his youth and early adulthood Germany had been so suffocated by nationalism that foreign travel was not encouraged.

Over the ensuing weeks they found ample opportunity to meet at parties. He told her that his mother was Swiss and that he had a Scottish great grandfather, enabling him to consider himself a cosmopolitan, even though he had never been outside Germany. Anton Knyphausen lacked Paddy's handsome bearing, yet he had the advantage, in Armgard's eyes, of being settled in one country and having made a niche for himself among a group of intellectuals whom she much admired. None of them needed to waste time with diplomatic small talk or to gossip about people and protocol. She thought about Anton during the daytime while she worked at her typing course, wondering how soon she could become a journalist alongside him.

Gradually he began asking her to join him at the theatre or his friends' houses. He seemed proud to be escorting a girl whose auburn hair shone like a halo round her head and whose eyes reflected wide horizons. Although her mother described her as skinny, Anton's friends admired Armgard for her elegance – more than that, she had a certain *je ne sais quoi* – a style – which drew admiring glances from men and women alike. They seemed the perfect match; each representing to the other a missing part of themselves. It was not long before he proposed. This time she found no reason to hesitate and gladly accepted his offer.

Soon Johan himself was back in Berlin, having completed his tour of duty in Brazil. He had come to take part in his daughter's wedding – a wedding for which he would pay the bill, yet one that had been entirely organised by his wife and her family.

'It was a grand wedding', Armgard told me. 'Many of my parents' friends came, and even my uncle Peter Michelet and our cousin Harriet were there from Norway. It took place on June 25th 1934, in the same church where I was christened; I was born and christened in Berlin because my parents met each other there – he was serving at the Norwegian Legation in Berlin at the time.'

'Have you any photos of your wedding?' I asked.

'No, they were all destroyed by bombs during the war. There are none left.'

As it turned out, she was wrong about that. After the death of my father, my mother developed an infinite capacity for discarding unwanted memories, both from her mind and in the form of books, mementoes – and photograph albums. 'It's just clutter,' she said when I reprimanded her. 'I don't need any of it'. On one occasion my son spent an evening in her London flat and, while helping her clear up after dinner, he tossed some rubbish into the bin. As he did so he noticed a dishevelled-looking book amongst the remains of food. When Sisi left the room he delved into the bin and pulled out a fabric covered photograph album which he later discreetly carried home with him. It turned out to be an important slice of family history. Pasted into the last few pages of the album was a photograph of Armgard's wedding, which became a useful piece of the jigsaw puzzle I was slowly putting together. It shows the wedding dinner at the Hotel Esplanade in Berlin. Sitting towards the front of the photograph, a young man wearing a swastika armband is looking into the camera. Who was he? I immediately sent a copy to Armgard's son, who recognised the man at once, although he had never before seen that photograph.

By now I had spent many hours getting to know Edzard, my only cousin on my mother's side, yet one who had been little more than a name in my life thus far. He told me he could never understand why my parents did not welcome him into their home or invite him to join their family celebrations – or why he was never part of my family, nor my brothers and I a part of his. In time I made him curious about his own parents and he readily joined me in the hunt for answers to the mystery. He had already started to research the war years and the part his father may have played, but now he was helping me on a wider investigation; we trawled wartime archives in many countries, read books about the war, studied memoirs and diaries and translated letters written in various languages. The slightest clue caused me to ring him and discuss its meaning. Even to Edzard, his father had always been something of an enigma. Yet, as we soon discovered, factual information dug up from Public Records offices in many parts of the world gives only part of the story. Personal memories were needed as well.

At Armgard's eightieth birthday party she introduced me to German cousins whom I had never met before, as well as some of her friends. I became engrossed by the stories they were happy to share with me, and asked them for yet more details. It did not take long to discover that, whereas one person remembered an event vividly, recounting it in detail, another might have a different interpretation of what happened. Of course this is nothing unusual. Most of us revise our biographies, ironing out the creases of awkward memories and then fervently believing the version we have created. My job was to find a consensus and to weave the many and varied stories into one continuous thread.

After Armgard and Anton's wedding service in the church, the bride and groom and all the guests gathered for a formal dinner at the Hotel Esplanade, one of the finest in Berlin. Omi's family, headed by Miriam, was there in full support. As was the custom, the gathering was limited to family and close friends; as well as a number of Anton's relatives, it included the Italian Ambassador and his wife, friends from Rio and Peking, and Lagi Solf, pleased to have been the matchmaker in this union.

Also among the guests at the dinner table, sitting next to Harriet Michelet on one side and his wife on the other, was Wolfram Sievers, who would later play an important role in both Anton and Armgard's life. For the moment – to my mind – he was simply the man wearing a Nazi armband. Although such armbands were a common sight in the streets of Berlin, it would not have pleased some of the older people in the room. Yet in the photograph he seems oblivious to this fact, as he proudly displays his allegiance to Hitler.

But the wedding dinner belonged to the bride and groom. From the beginning Omi took Anton Knyphausen, now her son-in-law, to her heart, having decided soon after first meeting him that he represented all that was best in Germany. And Miriam was

Armgard and Anton's Wedding Dinner.
Wolfram Sievers is nearest the camera on the right

happy that through Anton, Armgard had returned to the fold.

Johan Michelet, on the other hand, who had pinned such high hopes on his eldest daughter, showed his lack of enthusiasm for her choice by delaying his arrival in Berlin until a couple of days before the wedding. Wary of German nationalism and appalled by the route the country was taking under Hitler's stewardship, he was not pleased that his daughter would become, through marriage, a German citizen. During the wedding dinner he sat sandwiched between Ida Knyphausen, Armgard's new Swiss mother-in-law, and the wife of one of Anton's cousins, Furst von Knyphausen. He would have made delightful conversation in German to them both about this and that and nothing much at all. His smile and

Armgard's wedding: l-r Anton's father Graf Franz Knyphausen, Armgard,
Anton, and Omi

the close attention he paid to their every comment would surely
have charmed them. A consummate diplomat of the old school,
he knew when to hold his own likes and dislikes tightly in rein.

Johan's only consolation in the ensuing weeks and years was to
remind himself – and others – that although Armgard had married
a German, she did at least gain a title through marriage. She was
now the Gräfin (Countess) zu Innhausen und Knyphausen. Yet
this satisfaction alone could never quite compensate for the feeling
that his daughter had defied his wishes and in so doing aligned
herself with Germany and the regime of Adolf Hitler.

But Armgard was happy at last. She called her husband Apo, a
nickname bestowed on him in childhood.

I just loved our life in Berlin before the war. Apo was a journalist *with the grandest Berlin newspaper, but pay was little in those days. We rented a small flat near the centre of Berlin which my parents furnished for us. We had a nice maid living in who looked after Edzard when he was born one year after our marriage so could continue our life of balls, dinners and lunches at the Italian, Greek, French and Egyptian Embassies. At each party we had to leave a tip for the staff. Sometimes the tip we had to give was the last money we had until the end of the month. There were rumours of atrocities but everyone had a good time and pretended not believing them. No one was afraid of war. We never realised that we were at this time dancing on a volcano'**.*

★ The expression 'dancing on a volcano' was famously used by Gustav Stresseman (1878-1929), who helped Germany recover from hyperinflation in 1923 and steered it carefully through the Weimar years. Just before his death, he foresaw the Wall Street crash and said, 'Germany is in fact dancing on a volcano. If the short-term credits are called in, a large section of our economy would collapse'. Which of course it did, bringing the Weimar years to an end – and allowing Hitler a toe-hold on the country.

5

Sisi's Wedding 1934

Having made up her mind to dislike the city before she even arrived in Berlin, Sisi decided to journey around Europe for a week or two at a time, returning every now and again to assure her mother she was safe - and to check her mail. Unwilling to share her feelings with her mother or Armgard, she held tight to memories of Paddy and hoped he might write to her. If she received a letter, she told herself, she would reply at once, but only to recount stories of her travels. By the time the first letter arrived there was plenty to tell. She had been to Naples and the ruins of Pompeii. On another journey she visited Albania with her childhood friend, Trudchen, staying at the German Legation in Tirana with one of Omi's cousins.

It was soon after Armgard's wedding that Sisi received the letter that would change her life forever. In his memoirs, written after his retirement, Paddy wrote:

One evening in July 1934 I was sitting in my flat in Rome, writing one of my regular letters to Sisi. Almost before I realised what was happening, I found that I was asking her to marry me. Sisi has since said that the letter lacked something in passion. Be that as it may, it produced the right result; a few days later I had her reply and I can remember very clearly walking out of the Chancery Office into the Embassy garden to read her letter there.

It was not long after Sisi left Brazil that Paddy had been transferred to the British Embassy in Rome. Settling into his new job, he found himself on the periphery of a political crisis. Mussolini held the reins of power at an uncertain time and telegrams raced from Rome to London about *il Duce*'s intentions. As a relatively junior member of the team, Paddy stood by and watched Mussolini keep Sir Anthony Eden, the British Foreign Minister, waiting for an hour outside his office. Eden was enraged by this insult and the meeting was a disaster. Paddy wondered if it had been necessary for Eden to come to Rome; he could so easily have sent his Ambassador to that first meeting in his place. The Ambassador would not have been insulted at the long wait; it was, after all, just another part of his job. The ensuing discussions might then have been productive – even changing the course of history.

Ambitious and keen to learn, Paddy was fulfilled by his work and took part in the busy social life expected of a young diplomat in a foreign posting. He loved Rome and already spoke good

Italian. Yet, as he wrote, he knew something was missing from his life and found himself proposing to Sisi. After an exchange of letters with her parents, her father agreed to give Paddy his daughter's hand in marriage.

Paddy's parents, curious to meet their eldest son's foreign fiancée, invited Sisi to stay with them at their home in Scotland. Always cheerful and optimistic, Sisi accepted the invitation with joy, expecting to love them as much as she loved Paddy.

At the beginning of September 1934 Paddy met her off the train in Glasgow in his father's car and drove her along the banks of Loch Lomond, before climbing the hill known as the 'Rest and be Thankful' and cruising down towards Loch Fyne. As he turned through the gates of his home and then rounded one last corner to start the slow descent to the house, Sisi saw Ardkinglas for the first time. So completely had it mellowed into its surroundings, she thought it must have been there for hundreds of years. Surrounded by heather-covered hills and hidden from the road by a judiciously planted arboretum, it stood proud of Loch Fyne and looked down across the water towards the small town of Inveraray.

Sparkling in the sun, Ardkinglas had an ethereal quality quite unlike Stötterlingenburg, her mother's family home where she had spent her early childhood. Paddy had only briefly described his home, simply telling her he would take her to meet his family at their house in Scotland – where they spent the summer months.

'It's a castle', she gasped.

Paddy laughed, telling her it was only a house that was built less than thirty years ago; he had been at the party to celebrate

Ardkinglas House

its completion. He explained that she would be meeting his two brothers and his sister Tasia, but Rosemary, his favourite sister, was abroad with her soldier husband.

In Brazil Paddy had lived frugally on his Foreign Office salary, so nothing in his manner had prepared Sisi for what was obviously a wealthy family. But she was used to meeting new people of all nationalities and at every stage of the financial scale. She walked confidently up the stone staircase, glancing at stained-glass windows displaying the family crest.

Perhaps Paddy failed to warn her about the close-knit Scottish family she was about to encounter. Perhaps, after three years away from home, he had forgotten how different they were from the international set in Brazil. He simply hoped his family would make her feel at home – and a few of them did.

Paddy's mother, Amie Noble, was Irish and known to one

and all as 'Darling'. Even her children, and later her grandchildren and great-grandchildren, called her by this name. Brought up in Dublin at a time when Ireland was still part of Britain, she was the sixth daughter of a Protestant family. Her father, Samuel Waters, worked for the Royal Irish Constabulary as chief of the Special Crime Department. As was the custom, Darling was expected to wait for her older sisters to find a husband before launching herself into Dublin's social round. By the time she reached seventeen, her turn arrived. She encountered a young Dublin gentleman who pleased her. It must be supposed he felt the same way, because he soon proposed marriage. Throughout their entire courtship they were never allowed to be alone. Even for a walk in the garden, a chaperone was required. On the morning of their wedding one of her married sisters let her into a secret.

'After your wedding, when you are lying with your new husband in your bridal bed, something very strange will happen. But don't worry; you'll soon get used to it.'

Darling pondered briefly. She was sure it had nothing to do with babies, because she knew - or thought she knew - how babies arrived. During her childhood another five children were born to her mother and she had watched as the doctor climbed the stairs on the day of each new arrival carrying his ample Gladstone bag. It was in this bag, her sisters once told her, that each new baby was brought to the house. She had no idea what 'strange thing' might happen on her wedding night.

When the wedding festivities were over, Darling retired with her husband to a hotel room in Dublin. She dressed herself in the hand-embroidered Irish linen nightclothes her mother had provided – and waited.

'What he tried to do to me that evening was much worse than anything I could ever have imagined in my wildest dreams. I just screamed and screamed until he left', she told her grand-daughters many years later, wanting to protect them from similar shock.

The unfortunate young Irish bridegroom contracted influenza soon after their marriage – and died. Neither Dublin society nor her younger sisters appreciated having a widow on their doorstep, particularly one who was both beautiful and vivacious. By a stroke of fortune, Molly, one of Darling's older sisters, had married well and was living in London. Her husband's name was George Noble and she invited Darling to stay with them. It was through George Noble that she met his brother John, the quiet, intellectual son of Sir Andrew Noble, who was Chairman of Armstrong Whitworth, one of the largest and most successful companies in Britain at the time, employing over 20,000 people.

John Noble and Darling soon married. The marital bed obviously no longer daunted her, because Rosemary, their first child, was born in 1903. Though Darling, disappointed to have a daughter, consoled herself with the saying:

First a girl and then a son
Thus the world is well begun.

And indeed her next child, born thirteen months later, was a son. They named him Andrew after his grandfather, but his Irish nurse took one look at him and exclaimed, 'He's a proper little

Paddy'. From that day on, he was never called Andrew.

Unfortunately for Paddy, the enthusiasm Darling felt for her first-born son did not extend to spending time with him. She had other priorities, one of which was foreign travel. When he was only two months old, she went on a business trip to Japan with her husband. Returning six months later, she barely recognised the child and felt no strong maternal instinct towards him. To make up for this lack of affection she dressed him in the finest Irish linen and French lace, even commissioning a portrait of him wearing a handsome dress of white lace when he was three years old. She presented him with a hand-bound Bible to take to Eton and arranged house parties for his Oxford friends when he was on holiday from university. It was she who suggested that he sit the Foreign Office exam, and to please her, he did.

Paddy's father was kind but distant. Sir John saw to it that Paddy had all he needed materially. He also reminded his son each time the boy set off for a new term at school that his grandfather and namesake, Sir Andrew, had been top of every form in every subject from the day he started school in Edinburgh until he left to study engineering. Paddy did well at school and at Oxford, and sat his diplomatic exams with success; he passed eighth into the Foreign Office out of two hundred applicants. Yet however hard he tried, he felt he could not live up to the high standards expected of him by his father.

Paddy's cousin, Image Stewart, wrote me a letter.

My mother [Dorothy Noble] was always Paddy's ally - she thought his parents treated him disgracefully. For some reason they were scathing and dismissive of all he did and all he was. We knew that Johneen [Paddy's brother] was his father's favourite - they were very alike and Johneen found his mother's conversations boring. Michael [Paddy's youngest brother] was his mother's favourite.

But on this, her first visit to Ardkinglas, Sisi knew nothing of the emotional pitfalls in Paddy's upbringing. Besides, she was busy familiarising herself with her new surroundings. The house itself was much larger than Stötterlingenburg, and during that first day she had difficulty finding her way around unless Paddy was by her side. On her own she kept meeting new people who gave her incomprehensible directions.

'You'll find Paddy in the Morning Room.'

Or, 'Everyone's having tea on the Loggia'.

Paddy's grandmother, Marjorie Durham Noble, a Scots Canadian by birth, described the building of the house in her memoirs:

In 1905 my husband bought the Ardkinglas estate from the trustees of the Callander family. My husband and sons, being continually travelling on business, it was said of them by Lord Ridley 'The Nobles take all the best houses in Northumberland and then sleep on the trains.' After living in so many other people's houses for shooting, we were to enjoy one of our own.

The architect was Robert Lorimer, afterwards knighted for designing the Chapel of the Order of the Thistle in Edinburgh. It was a great feat to have built Ardkinglas in two years, electric lights, carpets down, etc. We ... went into the new house on the 16th April, a lovely day; the pipers played and the children followed in a kind of procession around the house. At night a great bonfire was lit, while the full moon sparkled. A more lovely evening could not be imagined.

Paddy was one of those children. He was three and a half years old. At the very same time that the gentle house was being constructed in its peaceful waterside surroundings, his grandfather was building *Dreadnought*, the prototype of a series of warships that went into action during the First World War.

After the carnage of that war, Darling became a pacifist. She devoured books on the subject and attended lectures. She never let an opportunity pass without doing her best to encourage others to her way of thinking. Gentlemen adored her company and listened to her eccentric ideas. Yet they noted, privately, that she liked the good things in life that came her way through the warships of her father-in-law.

The paradox that was Darling did not end there. She was outspoken, flamboyant and frequently caused embarrassment to her five children – yet she expected conformity from others.

On this memorable first evening of Sisi's visit, a family gathering sat around two Irish hunting tables for dinner. The ladies had changed into long gowns and jewellery. Sisi was grateful to her mother, who had insisted on pushing the budget beyond its limits when she took her daughter shopping for clothes in Oslo. With this visit to Ardkinglas in mind, Omi also lent her a double string of pearls to wear round her neck in the evenings. From her seat at the junior of the two tables, Sisi looked out over the loch, which lay mirror-still in the evening light, its calm surface only disturbed from time to time by a heron gliding low before diving

Amie (Darling) Noble, soon
after her marriage

for a fish.

On the other side of the loch lay Dunderave Castle. Sisi's dinner companion explained that Aunt Lily lived there and went on to say that he presumed she had read *Doom Castle* by Neil Gunn, a novel with Dunderave as its centrepiece. Sisi, who had never heard of Neil Gunn, did her best to compose an answer but soon realised that he was not so much asking a question as making a statement. Almost immediately he turned to the family member on his other side, leaving Sisi to flounder out of depth in their family chatter and gossip. Despite her many British friends in Brazil, whom she imagined to be typical of their counterparts back home, she struggled to find common ground for conversation; the Noble family and their guests showed no interest in her own wide world of experience and talked across her about people she did not know.

Aspiring always to be liked, Sisi saw herself reflected in the mirror of other people's behaviour. In Brazil the reflection she caught was one of approval; she knew the group of friends with whom she mixed liked her *joie de vivre* and were impressed by her ability to converse in many languages. From the faces of the dinner guests at Ardkinglas she glimpsed a different picture: the reflection showed her as a most unusual stranger in their midst. And yet she thought she could – in time – win them over.

After dinner the ladies withdrew from the table, leaving the men to enjoy port and cigars. Walking leisurely towards the drawing room, Darling turned to Sisi. In a sentence Sisi never forgot, her hostess, using a *sotto voce* that could be clearly heard by the other ladies, intoned, 'My dear, you really can't wear clothes like that here. Tomorrow we'll go to Glasgow so you can buy some suitable things for Ardkinglas.'

Sisi continued to put one foot in front of the other – but only from habit. At the end of the hall the ladies turned right into the drawing room. She drew away from them, holding down tears that were exploding within. Skipping any formalities she might have been expected to extend to her hostess, Sisi fled in the other direction, up the stairs to the safe haven of her room. Sleep was not an option while Darling's words kept piercing her thoughts and dismissing the peace that should have come with slumber. What was wrong with her long, deep-blue silk dress? Cleverly cut to show off her excellent figure, it would have been considered stylish in Rio or Berlin. It was true the ladies at Ardkinglas had worn more sedate dresses for dinner, dresses that seemed old-fashioned to Sisi. Why didn't Paddy warn her? As her mind wandered back to afternoon tea, she remembered how comfortable Paddy's sister and cousins had looked in their pleated tweed skirts with a matching jacket. She did not possess such an outfit. What was she to do?

Here in Scotland, Sisi had no one to turn to. Without funds of her own she was powerless. Rules of etiquette dictated that until the marriage had taken place it was inconceivable for a woman to ask her fiancé for financial help. After a long and lonely night, she faced her future mother-in-law at the breakfast table. Unwilling to demean herself even further by admitting to her lack of wealth, she pretended to be unwell, an excuse that served well enough to explain her drawn face and to turn down the offer of a visit to the fashion houses of Glasgow.

The sunshine that greeted her arrival had given way to a dense, misty rain which swirled up from the loch and clung resolutely to the hills, distorting their form and colour. As far as she could see the outlook remained grey. Paddy was thrilled; the weather was now perfect for fishing. Inviting her to join Michael and himself up the glen, he offered to show her how to catch a salmon and

Paddy and Sisi in the porch at Ardkinglas. Sisi realises that she is wearing the wrong clothes yet again

pointed to a rack of mackintoshes in the porch, telling her to borrow any one of them.

The well-intentioned invitation was turned down, as Sisi retired instead to the comfort of her room. Pulling a thick piece of writing paper from the stand on the desk, embossed with the words 'Ardkinglas, Cairndow, Argyll', she wrote to Armgard telling her that the house was very beautiful, and the Nobles had been nice to her. This was an early attempt to conceal her feelings – an accomplishment she perfected in the years to come.

Six weeks later, on 16th October 1934, Paddy and Sisi were married in one of the biggest churches in Oslo. Norwegian newspapers sent journalists and photographers to capture the couple on camera, both outside the church and later at the reception held in the Grand Hotel. The Michelet family was well known in Oslo and the ties between Norway and Britain had

Paddy and Sisi on their wedding day

never been stronger.

Paddy's parents attended the wedding, together with his sisters Rosemary and Tasia and brother Michael. During the wedding dinner in the hotel, Johan Michelet sat at the centre of the huge dinner table and beamed with pleasure. Although of course he would have liked his second daughter to have chosen a Norwegian husband, he was vastly relieved she had not followed Armgard's example by marrying a German. Not only was this young man

Sisi, Darling and
Armgard in Oslo
before the wedding

– now his son–in–law – a diplomat, Johan discovered he was also heir to a title, money and even an estate in Scotland. Paddy pleased him yet further by learning some Norwegian before the marriage and making all his vows in church, as well as an introduction to his after–dinner speech, in his host's language.

There was another guest who enjoyed every minute of the wedding: Paddy's mother, controversial as ever, went out of her way to talk to all the German guests. Having heard her husband and his friends discussing the threat of Germany's new economic strength and sensing a growing disquiet between the two countries on account of the new Chancellor, Adolf Hitler, she wasted no time in inviting herself to stay with Armgard and her husband in Berlin. Like a flash of lightning a new role had opened up for her. She would start to construct a bridge of peace and love between the people of these two countries.

Armgard was also happy. She noticed, right from the start, that if Paddy bore any grudge towards her for turning down his proposal of marriage, he did not show it. She watched with pleasure as Paddy and Anton conversed during the days leading up to the wedding. Paddy enjoyed speaking German and the two men had much in common. They were both quietly academic

Sisi's wedding: Paddy's sister Tasia is far left. Harriet Michelet is far right. On her left is Paddy's brother Michael.. Anton sits on the right, further away away from the camera

and seemed to outsiders to be at ease in each other's company. Both had fathers who remained distant from them. And both wanted to travel.

By one of those accidents of history that occurs across the boundaries of families and countries, Anton and Paddy were also linked by their forebears. Anton's grandmother was the daughter of the Scottish shipbuilder John Scott Russell, who worked alongside Isambard Kingdom Brunel on the design and construction of the *SS Great Eastern*; at the time of her launch she was the largest ship in the world.

The Brunel and Noble families were closely entwined – by friendship and by the fact that they twice intermarried. Paddy's father was named John Henry Brunel Noble in honour of Isambard.

Unfortunately Anton's great-grandfather, Scott Russell, and Paddy's family connection, Brunel, developed a rivalry as they neared completion of the ship. They fell out over matters of finance and over which of them should take most credit for the design of the ship. But history had the last word, decreeing that Scott Russell's name remains forever linked with Brunel in the catalogue of great engineering achievements.

In the second half of October 1934 Paddy and Sisi started their honeymoon by travelling from Oslo to Rome, which was to be their home for the next three years. On the way they stayed a few days in Berlin with Tante Sigrid and her husband. They also dined with Anton and Armgard in their small Berlin flat, allowing the sisters a chance to gossip about family and the wedding in Oslo, while the men discussed the German economy. It was plain to see that working-class people now enjoyed a prosperity they had previously only dreamed about; Paddy had already noticed how many of them owned their own *Volkswagen* (people's car) which sold at an affordable price, and how different the atmosphere was from his last visit to Germany in 1923.

The political situation, on the other hand, was probably not discussed. When Hitler became Chancellor in March 1933, his party gained enough power to enact laws without parliamentary approval. By the time Paddy and Sisi arrived in Berlin, Nazi Party members had control of every university, factory and public office, and had abolished both the Social Democrats and the Communists, imprisoning thousands for their political views. Narrowly avoiding arrest, the young Social Democrat, Willy Brandt – who in 1969 would become Chancellor of Germany – had already fled to Norway, changing his name and nationality to avoid retribution.

Hitler had also curtailed the liberty of the press and condoned the murder of Ernst Röhm, the leader of the Brown Shirts (the SA) and over one hundred of his chief officers. By then they had served their purpose in bringing Hitler to power and were becoming an impediment to his progress. This killing, known as the 'Night of the Long Knives', allowed the feared SS to step into their shoes. At the same time an intense campaign against Jews was growing daily, depriving them of their rights, their jobs and sometimes even their homes; three months before Paddy and Sisi arrived in Berlin, groups of Nazis had roamed the length of the Kurfürstendamm, the Champs Elysées of Berlin, wrecking Jewish-owned shops and attacking anyone they believed to be a Jew.

Like an elephant standing in the room, these matters were known to both Paddy and Anton, yet would have been a subject best skirted over or even avoided altogether.

While the honeymoon couple drove south towards Stötterlingenburg along *autobahnen* (motorways) that Hitler's government had so conveniently constructed, Sisi passed on the gossip she had recently heard from Armgard about Omi's family name: von Lambrecht-Benda. She told Paddy that her mother's great grandfather, Robert von Benda, had been Leader of the National Liberal Party in Parliament and a good friend of the Kaiser. As well as a wife and his son Kurt, Robert had a mistress whose name was Frau Lambrecht. She lived at Stötterlingenburg and when she died she bequeathed her estate not to her lover, but to her lover's son. There was, however, one condition. Kurt must add the name Lambrecht to his own, which of course he happily did; he and his wife Miriam moved into Stötterlingenburg just after Omi was born and lived there ever since.

As Paddy and Sisi drove up towards the gates of Stötterlingenburg she warned him that the von Lambrecht-Bendas – even her grandmother Miriam – were staunch Prussians, supporting Kaiser Wilhelm without question, even though he now lived in Holland. They also approved of Hitler, believing that he was restoring a sense of pride to the German people.

Arriving at the house, the honeymoon couple were greeted not only by Miriam, but also an exuberant gathering of young von Lambrecht-Bendas, all curious to meet the British diplomat who had married into their family. They showed pleasure in the fact that he spoke excellent German – and that he diplomatically voiced no disapproval of their country. Miriam proudly gave Paddy a tour of the house and garden.

'I hope one day soon you will have children and bring them here to see their mother's family home.'

The honeymoon continued in Budapest, where the couple held hands on Buda Castle and glanced across the Danube to Pest. In Pest they spent their evenings at a series of small restaurants around the centre of the city. Hungary was emerging from the austerity of the post-war era and celebrating in the way its people knew best: late into the evening gypsies serenaded the bridal couple with violins until the temptation to dance grew so intense that, along with other diners, they rose to their feet and waltzed. Their dancing had a new rhythm now, and a more settled pace, but the love that for Paddy had been nothing more than a flickering flame now gave him a warm glow and held them close. As they drove towards Rome to start a new life together, they planned their future, believing that nothing could mar their happiness from now on.

7

War Begins for Armgard 1938-40

I sent my manuscript for this book to my brother Tim. He helpfully corrected my mistakes on family matters and added a startling piece of information. 'Ewan Butler', he wrote, 'was Paddy's first cousin, the son of Darling's sister, Olive'. Butler is a fairly common surname, so I had never given it a second thought when I saw Ewan's signature in Armgard's Berlin guest book. But surely Armgard would have discovered the link? What could have been more natural before the war than mentioning to your English guest that your sister was married to a British diplomat? Ewan would then have asked for her brother-in-law's name, possibly adding, 'I have a cousin who is a British diplomat' and so the link would have been established and remembered.

Armgard never forgot details like that, so why did she refrain from mentioning it to me?

The first time the name Ewan Butler cropped up was on one of my periodic visits to Basel. Armgard allowed me to study the few photograph albums she inherited from her mother, and other books of memories. She seemed happy to elaborate on the stories behind them. One day I found a leather-bound book inscribed on the cover with the words *Unsere Gäste* (Our Guests), which dated from the years she and Anton lived in Berlin before the war. I turned the pages slowly while she enjoyed an afternoon nap. Here and there I recognised a name, but the page that caught my interest was headed '13th May 1938' and contained the signatures of some people who had by now become familiar characters in Armgard's stories. When Armgard returned to her salon, I asked her to describe that particular evening to me.

It was not long after Hitler annexed Austria, she told me. At that time many of their friends had started to shun foreigners living in Berlin because they often spoke out against Hitler and what he was doing. But Anton and Armgard were interested to hear what foreigners had to say and continued to invite them to their home.

The first person to sign her name in the guest book on that particular evening in May, and therefore probably the first to arrive, was Lagi Solf, who four years earlier had introduced them to one another – and who was still one of Armgard's closest friends. Slim and well dressed, she imbued any gathering with an aura of international sophistication.

Also on that guest list was an American, John Ratay, who had known the Michelet family when he served in Peking after the First World War. Although considerably older than Armgard, Ratay nevertheless remained in touch, and frequently dined at the Knyphausen's home. Posted to Berlin by his government to study records of German divisions that faced American troops in France during the First World War, he was also carefully watching the current disbursement of troops. One year after this party, he would be promoted to Colonel and meet up again with Anton and Armgard, in Bucharest.

Another name in the guest book for that evening was Helga Greene, the half-British, half-Norwegian wife of Hugh Carleton Greene – and a close friend and ally of Armgard. Both women were blessed with eye-catching auburn hair and they often strolled out into the park together with their young sons, Edzard and Graham; it was a perfect rendezvous for the two ladies, somewhere they could freely discuss world events and the politics of Germany as they perceived them, as well as comparing intimate stories about the joys and problems of motherhood. The Greenes and Knyphausens also dined from time to time as a foursome in each other's homes. A brother of author Graham Greene, Hugh had been the *Daily Telegraph* correspondent in Germany since 1934. Berlin at that time was a magnet for some of the best foreign correspondents in the world; they compared notes with one another, picked each other's brains, tried to sift true stories from an overload of propaganda and drank happily together in the evenings at an Italian restaurant called the *Taverne*.

Foreign correspondents tended to mistrust their German colleagues, some of whom were known to be government agents, but through the friendship of their wives, Hugh and Anton found common ground to exchange views and learn from one another. Hugh would meet up again with the Knyphausens two years later in Bucharest, before being recalled to London to take over responsibility of all BBC wartime broadcasts into Germany. Fifteen years after the war he went on to become Director-General of the BBC.

And then, on that same guest list, was the name Ewan Butler, who signed the book for himself and his wife Lucy. Ewan was acting chief correspondent in Germany for *The Times*. Armgard told me that he and Anton originally met through the network of journalists working in Berlin and soon the two couples became friends. Ewan, judging from what I have since read in his own memoirs and also in other histories of the period, was gregarious and convivial, and would have ensured that the conversation in the Knyphausen apartment that evening remained lively and provocative, no doubt entertaining the other guests with his views on the socialist regime in Germany and the failure of the British government to understand the problems that lay ahead. Being well travelled and a fluent German speaker, Ewan later received training as an SOE (Special Operations Executive) agent and served in Sweden during the latter part of the war – where he would once again meet Anton and Armgard. Did something occur in Sweden that caused Armgard not to mention to me – nor even to Edzard – the connection between Ewan and Paddy?

In July 1938, three months after that evening in Berlin, Anton's newspaper transferred him to Vienna. The family travelled by train, stopping en route in Stuttgart to stay with Anton's parents. Armgard had no wish to leave Germany, guessing rightly that they would not be welcomed by the Austrians. Once in Vienna, she missed her friends and the heady atmosphere of Berlin, where the dancing and entertainments still continued, despite disquieting rumours of trouble ahead.

In Vienna they found a pleasant apartment in the old Palais Hoyos in the centre of town, but no matter how hard she tried, Armgard never managed to feel at ease among the Austrians. Aristocratic families kept them at arm's length, making it clear they did not like Germans – even those with a title- and that they deeply resented what the German government was already imposing on Austria. At the same time many tradesmen, or people serving behind the counters in shops, showed themselves to be such staunch admirers of Hitler's National Socialism that Armgard found it embarrassing to talk with them.

Anton worked long hours, frequently disappearing from the city on missions that took him away from home for a few days at a time. Whereas in Berlin Armgard had friends and relations and therefore did not mind being left behind when he was called to work elsewhere, Vienna seemed even more unfriendly when she was on her own. She asked Anton questions about the articles he was writing; any form of journalism was of interest to her and these were particularly interesting times. After a while she began to notice discrepancies between the articles he wrote and the places he purported to have visited. It was not long before she discovered he was being unfaithful to her on his absences from home. She felt humiliated and jealous.

Added to her worries was the ever more troubling news heard each day on the wireless. Germany had sent troops into the Sudetenland. What would happen next?

On 30th September 1938, Armgard and Anton listened to Chamberlain's speech, made on his return to London after signing the Munich Agreement with Hitler, Edouard Daladier of France and Mussolini, who acted as mediator. From the steps of his aeroplane as he arrived back in Britain the next day, Chamberlain announced to the British people:

... we regard the agreement signed last night and the Anglo German Naval Agreement as symbolic of the desire of our two nations never to go to war again ... I believe it is peace for our time. And now I recommend you to go home and sleep quietly in your beds.

Yes, Armgard thought, on that count I can now sleep quietly.

Some months later she became alarmed when Edzard began to cough and lose weight. She took him to a paediatrician in Vienna who, to Armgard's distress, diagnosed tuberculosis and arranged for the boy to be sent immediately to Obersemmering, to a home for contagious children high in the hills above Vienna. At first Armgard made the arduous journey to visit him every day. Depressed by her separation from Edzard and the guilt she felt each time she left him on his own at the clinic, she realised that she had once again become powerless to control any part of her own life – even that of her sick son. Her husband continued to make trips around Austria, often for longer periods than was strictly necessary.

Five months after Chamberlain made his famous speech, Anton was ordered to serve with the German Wehrmacht as a private soldier and to take part in the march into Prague. On 16th March 1939 German forces quickly occupied the whole of Czechoslovakia and in so doing invalidated the Munich agreement, upon which the peace so tentatively hung. What did Anton see on this march? Serving with the elite Prussian Deutschmeister Regiment Nr 1V, wearing German military uniform, there must have been much to make a young man from a liberal background feel uncomfortable. Having spent nearly a year in Vienna, conversing often with foreign journalists, he would have questioned Hitler's right to annexe Czechoslovakia. He left no notes about that period of his life and none of his family heard him speak about it. Even Armgard never mentioned the march into Prague; it must have been one of those periods in the course of their life together that was best forgotten.

During his six-week absence, she continued to travel by train to visit Edzard. One day, while returning to Vienna, she found herself in the same compartment as a German doctor of about her own age. She learnt he had been abroad often on business and spoke with knowledge about the political situation in England and France. He laughed when she told him how uncomfortable she felt among the Austrians, telling her that they were only standoffish because she was perceived as German, whereas they despised him whether they were aristocrats or working class,

Anton in the uniform
of the Prussian
Deutschmeister Regiment

because in their eyes he was Jewish first and foremost, and only incidentally German.

They met up again in Vienna from time to time while Anton was away, enjoying a cup of coffee and *Sacher Torte*. Her need to talk with him, to feel his presence, became more urgent than any fear of what nosey neighbours might say about their relationship. As they became friends, she learnt that he was waiting for a visa to enter Argentina, as he felt life in Germany or Austria would always be difficult for a Jew, despite his medical qualifications. Armgard started visiting the sanatorium less often than usual, knowing that her time with the doctor was limited. Edzard felt her desertion deeply at the time and spoke about it with pain many years later. One day Armgard heard her friend utter the words she had been dreading. He would be leaving shortly for Argentina. She knew this moment had to come, yet was despondent at the suddenness of it. He suggested she might like to join him in Buenos Aires as soon as Edzard recovered; she would be able to attend university there, as she had always wanted, and Edzard could have a better start in life.

Many years later Armgard told Edzard that she met up with the doctor long after the war was over. He told her he had written her a letter as soon as he arrived in Buenos Aires, inviting her to join him. However by the time the letter arrived, Armgard had left Vienna and the letter was never forwarded.

After the occupation of Czechoslovakia by German troops, Anton was instructed to summon his family to join him. He was once again employed by the *Allgemeine Zeitung,* this time to cover news from Prague.

The Czechs were not welcoming and the Knyphausens faced even more intense hostility than they had known in Vienna – not without reason, as Armgard was well aware. Edzard had recovered his strength and sometimes, when they went out together to buy bread or vegetables, the shopkeepers refused to serve her if they heard her speaking German to her son. She yearned for the happy times in Berlin before the war, when life held so much promise and the rhythm of the dance held her close and safe in Anton's arms.

It was in the summer of 1939, while they were still living in Prague, that Anton was sent on a mission to Norway for four days. This time he asked Armgard to join him. Leaving Edzard with friends in Prague, she travelled ahead by train and boat. Anton, on account of his work, had been assigned a seat on an aeroplane to Oslo, where they met at her uncle's home. Uncle Peter and Tante Ella Michelet had a house in Frogner on the west side of town. Their daughter Harriet, the same cousin who had spent more than a year in Rio with Armgard and Sisi, still lived at home with her parents and would be company for Armgard.

Many years later Harriet described that visit. She said Anton left the house before breakfast each morning, with a large camera slung around his neck, returning exhausted each evening. As they ate dinner, Peter Michelet interrogated his young guest about the work he had done. Anton told him he had photographed the beautiful city and spoken to Norwegians. He always asked his host questions about Norway and smiled engagingly at his hostess, launching into accounts of his travels in Austria, which both Tante Ella and Harriet found amusing.

Like most Norwegians, Peter Michelet's loyalties lay with Britain. As he was normally a kindly man, Harriet was surprised by the icy politeness with which her father treated his German guest. Anton, who barely knew Uncle Peter, gave every appearance of accepting this behaviour as normal Norwegian formality. On his last day, Anton came into the kitchen where Harriet was making coffee, and discreetly opened his jacket to show her a swastika pinned inside the lapel. Only then did Harriet begin to understand her father's apprehension.

When I visited Armgard in Basel sixty years after this event, I mentioned the swastika to her. 'Harriet is quite wrong about that', Armgard retorted. 'I looked after all Anton's clothes and he never had a swastika on any of them. It was against everything he believed.'

Harriet, when I spoke to her again, was adamant she had seen it.

As so often happens with the passing of time, people subconsciously rationalise their memories to mould them to the shape of what they believe must have happened. We shall never know for sure whether or not Anton was wearing a swastika inside his jacket on that day. What we do know is that about ten months after the Knyphausens' visit to Oslo, Germany invaded Norway. Despite a spirited Norwegian defence and help from British battleships, German soldiers forged into Oslo, moving through the city as though they knew it well.

When, towards the end of the war, Anton sent Harriet a copy of the book he wrote in Sweden to show he disapproved of everything the Nazis stood for, he wrote on the fly leaf *'from your good friend Anton'*. But Harriet refused to read the book, saying she could never forgive him for what she saw as his treachery to Norway. Whether or not he was taking pictures of Oslo for military rather than journalistic purposes, she was convinced he had abused her father's house and facilitated the invasion. Anton must have realised later that the photographs he was asked to submit were probably information for a future invasion. Was the book he sent to Harriet his way of apologising?

Many months before that invasion of Norway, not long after Anton and Armgard's visit to the Michelets in Oslo, German troops entered Poland. Two days later, on September 3rd 1939, Britain and France declared war on Germany. They were joined by Australia, New Zealand, South Africa and India. Canada's parliament discussed the situation before opting, a week later, to fight alongside them. Immediately after the declaration, which Hitler announced was caused by 'British war inciters, intent on world conquest', Anton was transferred by his newspaper to Bucharest in Romania.

With joy in her heart, Armgard packed their belongings and followed him. Romania had declared its neutrality, which meant that she and Anton would be living in a country at peace. Renting a villa in an outer district of the city, they settled down to a new beginning, where Edzard could play safely in a public park with other children of his age. In Bucharest not only day-to-day food, but also luxuries, were still available, including caviar in abundance. As journalists from all over the world poured into Romania, a country where they could follow the progress of the war from a neutral safe haven lying close to the heart of the conflict, Anton and Armgard had the pleasure of meeting up with old friends.

Hugh Carleton Greene, still working for the *Telegraph*, was staying in the Athenée Palace Hotel in Bucharest while busily filing reports to London on the assassination of the Prime Minister,

Câlinescu, by members of the pro-Nazi party on 21 September. The killing had German approval and assistance, yet the media in Germany claimed that British and Polish agents had been the culprits. Hugh and Anton must have discussed this anomaly in private, yet Anton was forced to abide by Nazi propaganda in submitting his own articles. Hugh remained in Bucharest for two months, during which time they were able to catch up and exchange views.

Anton and Armgard also frequently visited the home of Colonel Ratay, who was now the American Military Attaché to Romania. It was through this Michelet family friendship, started in Peking and developed in Berlin, that Anton had access to the American Legation and its views on Hitler's campaigns. Although a staunch German patriot, Anton could see through the clouds of Nazi propaganda and began to question the statements of his own colleagues. Armgard enjoyed the chance to integrate freely with old friends and remain well informed on world events. Now that everyday life was enjoyable once more, their marriage seemed to take on a renewed warmth and companionship.

Encouraged by the sense of living in a fantasy world that might all too soon crumble around them, everyone they knew – Romanians and foreigners alike – seemed intent on enjoying themselves while the neutrality lasted, while fiddlers played in tune and music was still for dancing rather than propaganda. Cocktails at sundown, Russian caviar and roast pheasant killed after a day's hunting tasted all the better to those among them who understood the madness that was being unleashed all around them in one country after another.

Alas, as abruptly as it had started for Anton and Armgard, their stay in Bucharest was brought to an end. Someone at the German Legation in Bucharest decided to test the Graf von Knyphausen. It is possible that the diplomat's indignation was fuelled by a desire to please the Führer, but a more likely reason, since most diplomats were well travelled and tended to mistrust Hitler, was simply the diplomat's petty jealousy of Anton's inborn aristocracy and his ability to make friends and be informed by many different circles. The diplomat set a simple trap, inviting Anton to some spurious assignation – a trap into which Anton innocently slid. After a confrontation with the German diplomat and a denouncement of his treachery in front of the Minister, his journalist's pass was taken from him and he was ordered to return to Berlin within three days. On his arrival in Germany he was dismissed from his job on the newspaper. Armgard was yet again left to pack up their belongings and follow her husband.

Back in Berlin she made a valiant attempt to pick up the reins of her earlier life, but soon found that the city she had once loved with such passion had already lost its pre-war lustre. The restrictions imposed by the Nazis had blunted all but the most banal conversations and the atmosphere was already growing heavy with fear.

Anton, having been exposed to a view of the German leadership through the eyes of the international press and through his own experience of authorised deception and trickery, resolved to do whatever he could to bring down Hitler and his party. Yet he also had to feed his family and stay alive himself. His life would be difficult from now on.

Immediately after the war, when Anton was accused by the Swedish authorities of having once been a Nazi supporter, he denied the charge and wrote:

During the whole of this period (1939-1940) I knew Mr Hugh Greene - previously British journalist, now attached to the BBC sending out German language broadcasts. We knew each other in Berlin and Bucharest and, as his short letter to me will show you, he would hardly still remain a friend of mine if he suspected me of Nazi sympathies.

And in another letter:

I was in Bucharest. The Rumanian government wanted to give me an honour but the German Legation protested and did not extend my pass so I had to return to Germany within three days. I wanted at that time to escape to South America. An old friend of mine, the American Military Attaché, Ratay, was ready to get a false passport for me. The scheme did not work as I could not raise money for the flight.

In Berlin the *Abwehr* started an investigation for treason against Anton. He had no money and nowhere to live. Armgard realised they were at the mercy of the Nazis and totally dependent on any relatives who might be prepared to house them.

She began to feel the first cold grip of fear.

8

London 1938-39

Whereas Armgard found diplomatic life a strain, with its constant uprooting to another country and its veneer of flippant conversation, Sisi loved all that Paddy's career offered her; she was happy to be sent round the world whenever and wherever the British Foreign Office chose to relocate them.

They had been living in Rome for nearly three years by the time of my birth. Since Rome was not considered a suitable place, either medically or politically, for a confinement, Iain's birth had taken place in Berlin, where Sisi's family, including her mother, supported and cared for her. Two years later Sisi was pregnant again. Her father was then serving as Norwegian Minister to Finland, a country renowned for its excellent medical facilities. So

Paddy and Sisi at Ardkinglas
in 1938. Sisi knows that she is
now dressed appropriately

Omi was at hand again, not only to house Sisi before and after my birth, but also to help look after Iain. Armgard came to stay with her parents while Sisi was giving birth to me, enjoying the chance to introduce her young son Edzard to Iain and taking them off to the park to play together while Sisi nursed her newborn child – a child who had been given a Finnish name, Laila, in honour of the country where she was born. After a month to recuperate from my birth, my mother brought her two children back to Britain. By then Paddy had been recalled from Rome to work at the Foreign Office in London.

Together they set up home in a large house in Carlisle Square, on the western side of fashionable Chelsea. Sisi quickly made English friends, often ladies like herself who had travelled widely. Soon she was invited to their homes, learning to enjoy

The Noble brothers and sisters stand in order of age
r-l: Rosemary, Paddy, Johneen, Tasia and Michael

life alongside the quiet unflappability of Londoners, after so many years with the volatile Brazilians and Italians.

Now they had their own home, Paddy embellished it by bringing down a few good pieces of furniture and silver from Ardkinglas. When Paddy's father, Sir John Noble, died in 1938, he left the Ardkinglas estate jointly to his three sons, a most unusual distribution in those days, when estates were generally bequeathed wholly to the eldest male. If Paddy found his father's will hurtful, he never in his life said so. Perhaps on account of his diplomatic career, perhaps because Sisi found the Scottish climate too cold for her liking, or maybe simply to escape from the difficulties involved in sharing a property, he told his brothers that he did not want to live at Ardkinglas, and accepted a modest amount of money in return for handing over the house and his share of the estate to the two of them.

Soon after their arrival in London my parents hired a nurse to look after Iain and me. They had discussed whether it would be better for us to grow up speaking English and German or English and Norwegian. Deciding that German would be the more useful language of the two, they hired Schwester Olga, a trained children's nurse from Berlin, to ensure we would be bilingual in English and German.

And then, when Iain was only four years old, the world went to war.

9

War Begins for Sisi 1939-42

No sooner was war declared than Paddy and Sisi put Schwester Olga onto a boat headed for Germany, leaving Sisi to take on the role of full-time mother. Motherhood appealed to her; she had breast-fed both her children for six months – something no self-respecting British lady dreamt of doing in those days – and now she looked forward to spending time in the nursery.

But the war laid another imposition on Sisi which, unlike caring for her children, discomforted her. She was expected to deny her German roots. Until then, despite the British passport she acquired on marriage, she considered herself a *weltburger*, a citizen of the world. But now she was expected to give her loyalty to one country and one country only. Determined to be a good wife to Paddy, she gradually reinvented herself as a British person, pretending to her friends and even to herself that it was easy. On the rare occasions she dared bring up the subject of her mother she described her as 'Norwegian', a label she knew her mother would have deeply resented.

She gave up speaking German to us, and spoke Norwegian instead. She quickly discovered, however, that any unknown language made Paddy's friends uneasy. 'What's that foreign language you're speaking? Is it German? It sounds just like it to me.' Sisi wanted her children to grow up bilingual – as she had – but patriotism was sweeping the country like a wave of religious fervour, laying a hint of suspicion on all who were slow to follow its blatant anthem, forcing her to bury yet another part or herself and to speak only in English.

At the beginning of 1940, knowing they might soon be sent to a foreign posting, Paddy and Sisi engaged a new nurse. Born the same year as Sisi, Peggy Lambley had lived all her life in Yorkshire. As soon as she settled into the house in Carlisle Square, Peggy imposed a strict discipline over the nursery and brought a sense of routine to all the domestic duties under her charge. The whole family loved her from the very beginning.

In March 1940 Paddy was offered a posting to Shanghai as First Secretary at the British Embassy. He hesitated before giving an answer. Sisi was determined to follow him wherever he was posted, but he knew that life in China might become dangerous.

Japan needed *Lebensraum* – or, as they saw it, an empire – in which to house its growing population and develop some economic prowess. With that in mind, Japanese troops were slowly but inexorably tightening their grip on China. Only two years previously, working their way slowly down the country from the north, capturing Peking as they went, they stormed the then capital, Nanking (now Nanjing), raping women and slaughtering more than 260,000 Chinese civilians.

Yet the international concessions in Shanghai, according to everything Paddy read, were well guarded by British soldiers and would remain safe. He also knew that Sisi would be more at ease in China than in Europe, not only because she already knew China from her youth, but also because her family loyalties would be less stretched in faraway Shanghai.

After consulting Sisi, he asked Peggy if she would undertake the long journey with them. To his great delight she accepted with enthusiasm, saying that she had always wanted to travel and that China sounded 'just the sort of place' for her.

On 8th April 1940, as they were packing to leave for Shanghai, German warships cruised into Oslo, disgorging seven army divisions in 48 hours. Within days the troops moved inland to occupy all the main Norwegian ports. Paddy wrote: 'There could hardly have been a more inauspicious send-off for our trip to China'.

Paddy and Sisi, along with their two small children and Peggy Lambley, boarded the *Empress of China*, probably the last ocean liner to burn coal. When we stepped down the gangplank onto the Bund in Shanghai nearly a month later, we arrived in a city enriched by international trade and made famous by its glamour, greed and squalor. About 35,000 foreigners, many of whom by then considered Shanghai to be home, were still busy enjoying the things they had always done best: making money and having fun. The original British Concession, which included Australians, Canadians, New Zealanders and South Africans, had joined forces with America to create the International Settlement, where Chinese residents lived alongside the foreigners, all of them abiding by an administration of justice and tax laws in which Chinese officials played no part.

This unusual arrangement had been in place since 1842, when British merchant ships bringing opium to China were joined by naval vessels to fight and defeat the Chinese. The resulting Treaty of Nanking – an unequal treaty in the eyes of the locals – forced China to open five of its major ports to foreign trade and allow foreigners to live in concessions under their own rule of law. In Shanghai the British were soon joined by French, Japanese and American settlers; each country leased its own area from the Chinese government. Although this foreign domination of a large part of the riverside was still resented by locals, the Westerners thrived and soon modernised the city, introducing electricity, trams and radio stations, as well as turning the city into an important commercial centre that attracted trade and investors from all parts of the globe. Even the Chinese prospered, some more than others, taking advantage of the opportunities available. The exceptional harbour facilities of the Huangpu River enabled every sort of merchandise to be unloaded. The now-historic European buildings along the Bund were built by successful foreign companies and individuals who had made Shanghai their home.

Now, as war progressed, refugees flooded into the concessions, among them Chinese families from the north who had been left homeless by Japanese invaders, and countless Jews fleeing the ever-worsening persecution in Nazi-controlled countries. By the end of the war the number of non-Chinese residents in Shanghai had risen from 35,000 to an estimated 150,000.

While Japanese troops quietly commandeered large areas on the outskirts of the city, the Noble family moved into a European-looking house with an imposing garden, number 33 Rue Prosper Paris, in the French Concession, which was one of the best residential areas in town. The rolls of barbed wire laid down by Japanese troops to denote their newly taken territories were conveniently out of sight of the house.

Sisi arranged the furniture as Paddy liked it, settled Peggy and the children into their new regime and made sure Peggy was offered opportunities to make friends. Then she launched herself confidently into Shanghai society. A vibrant international community of old China hands welcomed her into their midst. There were parties to attend, gala events at the racecourse (now Renmin Park - the People's Park) and the Amateur Dramatic Society, which drew large numbers of foreigners to its productions. Sisi also busied herself helping to organise a series of charitable events. There were 9,000 British citizens in Shanghai in 1940, none of them paid income tax and most were happy to contribute large sums of money to the Allied war effort.

The Noble's house in the French Concession

Although Japanese planes had already directed aerial bombardment on civilians, they carefully avoided the international concessions. It is hardly surprising that whenever the looming Japanese presence came up in conversation, there was always someone ready to chant, 'Don't worry. The worst never happens in China'. And, in the beginning, the Nobles had reason to feel secure. The police in the International Settlement were under British command. There were still two battalions of British troops, the Seaforths and the East Surreys, as well as a battalion of the American 4th Marines, a detachment of Italian marines from the Battaglione San Marco- and various French troops in the French Concession.

Unlike other newcomers to Shanghai, Sisi felt at home at once. Having spent eight years in Peking, she still spoke some

The family together in their Shanghai garden

Mandarin and understood the customs that existed amongst the servants who ran her house. They included Number One and Number Two Boy, two cooks, an amah who did the washing and sometimes helped with the children, a coolie to do the hard work, the chauffeur, and a nightwatchman whose main duty was to open the gates when the family arrived home at night. The gardener looked after the garden, except for menial jobs such as weeding the lawn, which was done by a team of 'weedy women', whom he brought in whenever the need arose. Although they all earned small salaries, they were business people at heart and

A day at the races, a photograph taken by Paddy.
Sisi in a spotted dress, Iain, Peggy and Laila

knew how to make a living: they collected a kind of import duty
for everything they bought for the house, whether it was food
or petrol or feather dusters, and they fed a whole community of
friends and relations in the kitchen. It was all part of the game. Sisi
was also used to the custom whereby she sometimes found herself
eating with someone else's silver cutlery. On other occasions, when
attending formal dinners in the mansion of some businessman, she
would notice her own china or glass on their table. One evening
Sisi and Paddy were invited to dine with Philip Broadmead, the
Counsellor at the British Embassy. As the passenger lift was not
working, they came up in the service lift. Walking in through the
kitchen, they found their own cook preparing the Broadmeads'

dinner. Sheepish smiles were exchanged by everyone, but nothing was said.

Sisi was beginning to enjoy herself all over again. Amid the melting pot of foreigners in Shanghai, she knew she was perceived as a person in her own right.

Only a few months after their arrival, however, a visible reminder of the looming war cast menacing shadows over their good life. Paddy and Sisi watched as British troops left Shanghai for active duty in Singapore. Two battalions marched out over Garden Bridge to the accompaniment of the American 4th Marines playing 'Will ye no come back again'. Without any attempt to hide their interest, Japanese soldiers stood on the sidelines as the British troops departed. Whereas foreigners had always felt relatively secure, now even old China hands were beginning to keep a ready sum of cash to hand in case of a hasty exit.

Paddy and Sisi did their best to carry on as normal. Sisi ignored the distressing news she read in the newspapers and pretended it was not happening, while Paddy kept the contents of telegrams from London strictly to himself.

After Paddy's arrival in Shanghai, the British Ambassador, Sir Archibald Clark-Kerr, and his Counsellor, Philip Broadmead, followed Chiang Kai-Shek and his Free Chinese Government to Chungking, (now Chongqing), where the politicians had set up their headquarters and created a new capital city. Suddenly Paddy became the most senior British diplomat in Shanghai, with the responsibility for dealing with all local political and trade matters.

The British Embassy offices occupied the top floor of the

Jardine Matheson building on the Bund. Next door to it the Glen Line building, also British owned, had leased space to the German Consulate, which flew a Nazi swastika from the roof. Under the conditions then prevailing, it would have been impossible to remove the flag without starting a major and futile row with the Japanese, who by now had taken over about half the International Settlement.

Sisi, going out of her way to help Paddy cope with the everyday stress and traumas of his job, showed him an outward expression of unqualified love and respect that had never been offered him by anyone else. That, and the few brief hours he spent playing in the garden with his children, gave him the strength to carry on with equanimity.

The instructions from Europe did nothing to ease his workload – or his anxiety. Although no one in Shanghai doubted the ability of the Japanese to take yet a further slice of the city, orders from London insisted that two British gunboats depart for duties in Hong Kong. Paddy consoled himself by looking out of his office window to see the one remaining British gunboat moored in the Huangpu River alongside the Bund. *HMS Petrel* was on full alert.

Day by day, the Japanese were closing in. Since they had control of many Chinese ports, and occupied a part of northern Indo-China, they could progressively block off the shipping routes on which Chinese and European trade depended.

In September 1941, Paddy made the arduous journey to Chungking to confer with his Ambassador. He took a small Jardine coaster to Hong Kong and then an aeroplane from Kai Tak to

Chunking, landing on the perilous strip that straddled a pebble island in the middle of the Yangtze. The town itself was perched on steep mountains either side of the murky waters of the river. He stayed for two months. To get from his lodgings to the main part of town he descended precipitous steps to the river, crossed the water in a wheezing, overcrowded ferry and then climbed an equally steep flight of steps. The visit was tiring and did little to put his mind at rest. To add to his discomfort, Japanese aircraft were bombing the city. Fortunately the mountains made flying perilous, so most of the bombs failed to reach their intended targets.

Paddy was only thirty-eight years old, but by the time he returned to Sisi and his family in Shanghai he looked haggard and complained of headaches. The following day he was diagnosed with shingles and retired to bed.

He was still recuperating when, on Sunday December 7th, Japanese aircraft made a surprise attack on the American Navy at Pearl Harbour in Hawaii, then moved swiftly in Shanghai to sink *HMS Petrel,* killing many of its crew.

At 5.30am – the time difference meant that it was already December 8th in China – a phone call from the Embassy woke Paddy. Before driving into town he gave Sisi instructions to wake Peggy and the children, to pack their most valuable possessions and some clothes into suitcases and come to the safety of the

Embassy as soon as possible. Sisi, understanding him so well, knew at once that the calm demeanour he had shown for so long had been replaced by a controlled terror.

Reaching the office, Paddy oversaw the burning of all sensitive files – not an easy task, since speed was vital. Many bundles refused to burn, so individual papers were inserted one by one into the fire. However, instead of burning, some floated up the chimney in a half-readable state and drifted like large, dirty snowflakes down onto the Bund, causing Paddy to send a team of Embassy staff scurrying into the street to retrieve them. Later in the morning an official from the Japanese Consulate arrived to notify Paddy that a state of war existed between their countries and gave him two hours to close the Embassy.

Heavily guarded by Japanese soldiers, British and Dutch diplomats were herded into the Cathay Hotel (now the Peace Hotel), where they were to occupy the two upper floors of the building. Their families joined the men – Sisi, Iain, Peggy and me among them. From the windows we looked down on the Bund and watched the Japanese presence grow daily. Troop and supply ships were already sailing into town, boosting the confidence of Japanese soldiers as they strolled along the banks of the river; Chinese residents now walked to one side, keeping out of their way.

Like a caged animal, six-year-old Iain rode a bicycle round and round the corridor of the hotel that housed the eclectic group of prisoners. They were all in the same boat, Consular staff and Embassy guards, nannies and senior diplomats, playful children and frightened wives. Anyone with a skill to share gave lessons; Paddy taught his colleagues to type, being one of very few men of his generation who had made the effort to master that skill. Sisi played endless games of bridge with anyone willing to learn, even though her knowledge of the game was basic by any standards. The games helped pass the time for all those who joined her and, although the only two packs of cards soon became bent at the edges from overuse, the rubbers of bridge continued. Peggy scooped up all the children and conducted a school of sorts, using the flat roof of the building as a classroom when weather permitted.

When, many years later, Sisi was asked to describe the conditions under which we were held, her only comment was that Japanese guards were kind to children and that everyone had more or less enough to eat. She had by then purposefully forgotten the atmosphere of fear that hung in the air. Although all the families interned in the Cathay Hotel were covered by diplomatic immunity, no one knew how long the Japanese would honour that international convention. They had already shown themselves perfectly capable of taking matters into their own hands, in some places separating men from the women and in others committing heinous crimes, such as the brutal horrors in Nanking and other Chinese cities.

For four long months the families remained in the hotel with no news whatsoever from the outside world. Then, as if by a miracle of good fortune, they were told they would all be transferred to the Cathay Mansions in the French Concession.

Because the Vichy government in the south of France had collaborated with Germany, French nationals in China had permission to conduct their own affairs; they were considered allies of the Japanese. It was the French officials who insisted that the foreign diplomats be moved into their concession, and once they were safely installed, the French went further, demanding that the internees have a more liberal regime. Soon we were allowed to walk around certain areas of town during daylight hours, subject to conditions that varied from time to time according to the whim of the Japanese guards.

To Paddy and Sisi's great joy, a group of American internees joined us in the Cathay Mansions, bringing along a radio and much good humour. Although listening to the radio was forbidden, the guards generally looked the other way when prisoners switched on. For another four months, boosted by the arrival of the Americans, and able once more to find out what was going on in the world, we sat and waited.

Not that there was much consolation to be gained from the news. Singapore, a strategically important military base, well guarded by Allied troops, had fallen on 15 February 1942. A speedy and savage Japanese campaign had taken the overconfident Allies by surprise; Paddy and Sisi recalled with sadness the British soldiers who had left Shanghai two years earlier. Perhaps it was fortunate that at that stage none of them could imagine the horrors those men were to suffer.

With the help of French Embassy staff in Shanghai, plans were now being made to transport this large group of international diplomats and other foreigners to Africa, where they would be exchanged for Japanese diplomats. On 17th August 1942, along with British Embassy and Consular staff and as many members of the international community in China as could find their way on board, the Nobles and Peggy were unceremoniously piled into a Japanese liner, the *Kamaru Maru*, and transported to Lourenço Marques (now Maputo), the capital of Mozambique. Although aware that the journey itself would be fraught with danger, they all knew it was their best chance of getting out of China alive.

Flying a Red Cross flag, and with all lights blazing to denote that the ship was not engaged in military activities, the *Kamaru Maru* trudged through Asian waters. Despite those precautions, we narrowly missed being sunk in Singapore while loading supplies. On board were 810 passengers from Britain, Poland, Holland, Switzerland, Norway, Czechoslovakia and Greece. They had come from Shanghai, Tientsin, Peking, Harbin, Canton and Tokyo. The accommodation for many passengers was nothing more than a hammock slung in a corner of the storeroom, while Paddy and Sisi were fortunate enough to have their own cabin with extra mattresses on the floor for us. However, nobody complained; everyone on board knew they were fortunate to have this opportunity to reach some sort of safety.

Their arrival in Lourenço Marques brought a sigh of relief. Standing on terra firma, wondering where fate would carry them next, they gathered in groups, waiting to be given instructions. Paddy, Sisi, Peggy, Iain and I were among the throng of ill-fed passengers. Suddenly, from behind a barrier where well wishers and local onlookers stared at the unloading of this strange human cargo, a voice called out to us.

It was Darling, Paddy's mother. Now a widow and still a staunch pacifist, she was determined to put as much space as possible between herself and the war, leaving Britain in 1940 with all her jewels in a cloth bag, to settle in Japan, where she had contacts. After the bombing of the US fleet at Pearl Harbour she moved to Singapore. Soon afterwards the Japanese attacked that city. Darling made a hasty escape, saving her life but losing her much-loved jewels. Not one of them was ever found again. She settled in Africa – in Swaziland. Despite the distance from Britain and her unusual existence, she managed to keep contact with her family and somehow got word from the Foreign Office that Paddy and Sisi were being transported to Mozambique. There was nothing she enjoyed more than a useful adventure, so she quickly uprooted herself from her temporary home in Swaziland to make the journey to Lourenço Marques, where she rented a small house in the hills above the city and waited for their arrival.

Pushing through the barrier, she strode across the tarmac to greet us. Japanese sailors who tried to stop her were dismissed with a wave of her arm, while Paddy, torn between embarrassment and admiration, hugged his mother.

Darling had commandeered transport to whisk us away to her house some miles from the harbour. Paddy stayed overnight, but returned to town next morning to deal with the administrative nightmare of ensuring that each member of the British Commonwealth contingent was helped to find passage on board a boat headed roughly in the direction they wanted to go.

Sisi settled down in her mother-in-law's house, relishing the break from the overcrowded ship, the storms at sea and the endless bowls of rice. Darling, controversial as ever, recounted to Sisi her adventures since they had last met.

Before the war started, she had travelled to Berlin where she stayed with Armgard and Anton. She told Sisi she had written *'Ich liebe Berlin und alles Deutscher mensch'* (I love Berlin and all Germans) in their guest book. Her German was atrocious and Sisi could not help herself from laughing, but at the same time she felt closer to her mother-in-law than she ever would have believed possible.

'I shall go back to stay with Armgard when this terrible war is over', Darling assured Sisi.

She also listened to Sisi's stories of their life in Shanghai and treated Peggy as an equal. The three of them sat in the shade of palm trees to reflect on the wisdom of world leaders and the pity of war.

Though Paddy would never be completely at ease in his mother's company, Sisi found common ground with Darling during those two quiet weeks in Africa, and by the time the family set sail for Britain a mutual respect had developed between them. In many ways Sisi was sad to leave, uncertain what would be in store for her in Britain.

Arriving in Liverpool on board a P&O troopship, the *Narkunda*, we made our way on crowded trains to Scotland, where Paddy's brother Johneen and his wife Elizabeth stood waiting to welcome us at the front door of Ardkinglas. Johneen's first reaction when his brother climbed down from the car was a gasp of horror. Paddy, a man of average height, had always been well built, but the figure who emerged from the car was little more than skin and bone. He weighed eight stone (112 pounds/51 kilograms).

The Noble family at Ardkinglas, and the refugees from Belgium who lived with them, had eaten sparingly over the last few years; many staple foods were rationed, and others unavailable. But they always had enough to fill their stomachs. It shocked them to see Paddy, Sisi and their children arrive in such a visibly undernourished condition. After a few home-made meals of lamb stew with potatoes and carrots from the garden, Paddy perked up considerably. But he never spoke of his ordeal. The most he would do was make a joke of it: 'Before we were interned I had an overdraft at the bank. Now we are home I've got an underdraft. The Foreign Office kept paying my salary and I couldn't spend it'. Always one to talk about what he knew and never about what he felt, he barely mentioned his incarceration. However, he wrote a brief couple of sentences about the first night of his return to Ardkinglas, which goes a little way to understanding his nervous state:

Sisi and I slept in the Lily Room and I remember that when I awoke next morning, I was startled to see a fleet of ocean liners lying off Inveraray - until I discovered they were troop ships loading an American Division for the North African Landing. China and the Japanese were truly behind us.

Ten days later Paddy reported for work in London. He had been assigned to serve as the Foreign Office representative on the Joint Intelligence Staff (JIS), a privileged assignment that would involve working in Churchill's Cabinet War Rooms. The Foreign Office knew that Paddy's brother-in-law was German, yet they failed to pass this information to other members of the JIS. Whether this omission was simply an oversight, or whether it was because they had a reason for wanting Paddy in that job and knew he would be unacceptable with German connections, we shall never know.

10

The Knyphausens in Berlin 1940-41

Two years after my husband's death I had the good fortune to dine with my cousin Kate How and her husband in London. It was in their house that evening that I met an Australian and lost my heart. After a certain amount of long-distance travel between the two countries, we decided to marry. Thus I began a new life, spending a large part of each year in Melbourne. Armgard wrote in her first letter to Australia:

So you are now living with your new husband in a new country. I know little about Australia except for their tennis players who are good at winning. You must write to me about the life there, I would like to learn about it.

Our correspondence began in earnest. Soon I amassed

a huge folder bulging with her precious letters. She loved her ancient typewriter, writing quickly to fill each page before adding handwritten notes in the margins. She often changed subject midstream, sometimes even in the middle of a paragraph, sometimes with barely a full stop to guide me onto the new tramlines of her thought. I looked forward to each letter, tearing open the envelopes as soon as they arrived.

But it was on my visits to her home in Basel that I learnt the most. While I was with her we talked all day long – in her kitchen while she prepared food, sitting on her small balcony or as we walked out into the street to buy groceries. During meals or at any other time it suited him to do so, her husband joined us and then the talk centred on him. It was after all his home, so I held back my feelings of resentment at his intrusion and listened to his views of French history or the benefits of a Swiss lifestyle. When Armgard and I were on our own, everything she had to say was important to me.

At this stage in our relationship I had no reason to suppose she was withholding information. Her stories flowed easily. I asked questions but had learnt never to probe. When she chose not to elaborate on a story by hastily changing the subject, or giving me a cloudy answer that left me none the wiser, I had no heart to push further. Since she tended to jump frequently from one subject to another, from the history of China to today's news on the radio – or from stories of life in Berlin during the war to questions about London art galleries – it seemed that my most important role was to put her story into chronological sequence.

Returning from Romania to Berlin in early 1940, Anton considered his future. The case against him for treason had been dropped but he had no income, no immediate prospect of a job and no home. His first priority, to put a roof over their heads, was not straightforward. Schloss Remseck, his family home, boasted many bedrooms, a better climate than Berlin and a large garden where Edzard could play. But Anton had never been close to his father and had no wish now to be dependent on him. Not that the Graf Franz zu Innhausen und Knyphausen could have helped his son financially. Although the Remseck estate had once been prosperous, earning a good income, Franz was now burdened with debts and had sold much of his land to neighbours, keeping only one farm to bring in a small income. Wrapped in his own problems, he allowed yet more money to slip through his fingers. His wife never complained, merely withdrawing herself from him emotionally until he, further exasperated by the rejection, began to bully her. Anton loved his mother dearly but had no idea how to help her and, besides, he needed to stay in Berlin in case one of his contacts in the world of journalism found work for him. He turned instead to his sister for help.

To the great relief of both Anton and Armgard, Gerda and her husband invited them to stay. Although they too had a child to look after, and their home in the centre of Berlin was not large, they made room for Anton, Armgard and Edzard. From the start Gerda made her sister-in-law feel at home. Together they cleaned the house and cooked meals, and in the evening, once the children were in bed, they drew the curtains against prying eyes and ears before settling down for a chat. Gerda was married to a lawyer, Richard Kuenzer, a German diplomat working as *Legationsrat* (Counsellor) at the Foreign Ministry. For some years already Richard had been involved with the opposition to Hitler. At one stage it was relatively easy to hold secret meetings without fear of being caught, but with each passing month the eyes and ears of the Nazi faithful became more and more intrusive. Richard knew the dangers he courted, but felt strongly enough about his beliefs to risk not only his own life but also those of his wife and daughter. Anton offered to help his brother-in-law in any way he could.

Gerda and Armgard discussed quietly with one another the dilemma facing many decent Germans; they had the choice of ignoring the ever-worsening tactics of Hitler's regime, in the hopes it would somehow end of its own accord, or of endangering their family by opposing it. Whereas Norwegians who were already defiantly resisting their Nazi occupiers were considered heroes in their own country, and were quietly aided by friends and neighbours, Germans in Germany who opposed the regime were ostracised and labelled unpatriotic. There was no shortage of neighbours in Berlin willing to report unpatriotic behaviour to the Gestapo, and the gruesome consequences of a betrayal were enough to deter most people from joining anti-Nazi groups.

For the moment the Knyphausens and the Kuenzers lived relatively well. Though many food items were already unavailable,

Lagi Solf's wedding to Count Ballestrom in 1940. Anton stands with his back to the camera, talking to the bride, Armgard is in a fur hat behind him

they were not yet hungry. Allied Embassies had closed their doors; Anton and Armgard no longer went to parties but still enjoyed an occasional quiet dinner with old friends and attended Lagi Solf's wedding to her second husband.

After several months of hospitality at the Kuenzers' home, they felt bound to move on, finding lodgings in a series of guesthouses in Berlin. Lack of income soon forced them to seek cheaper alternatives and they stayed for a while with Miriam at Stötterlingenburg, before returning to Berlin, where Anton at last managed to find some freelance work. This involved travelling to different parts of Germany, allowing him at the same time as writing his articles to pass messages for his brother–in–law.

Armgard never asked where he had been. It could have been dangerous for both her and Edzard had she known.

Since Anton was away so often and money was short, in the spring of 1941 Armgard took Edzard to Stuttgart to stay with Anton's parents. His mother, Ida, had been ill for some time and Armgard offered to help look after her in any way she could.

Ida Knyphausen, the daughter of a Swiss father and a Scottish mother, too ill by now to cope on her own, welcomed Armgard's presence during those last months of her life. She and her husband were barely on speaking terms, so her only close companion in recent months had been the housekeeper. Armgard's arrival gave her the opportunity to pour out her feelings. She reminisced about her international childhood and early married life, unburdening to Armgard the disaster that befell her inheritance.

After the death of Ida's maternal grandfather, John Scott Russell, the Scottish shipbuilder who made a fortune alongside Brunel on the building of *The Great Eastern*, a substantial sum of money was left to Ida's mother. When her mother died this money came to Ida. However, at the time of her marriage to Franz Knyphausen, he proposed that her capital should be taken out of the Swiss bank account where her mother had lodged it and invested in Germany, where he could keep an eye on it for her. During the hyperinflation of 1923 her entire inheritance melted away – leaving her penniless and vulnerable. When Armgard explained that her mother had also lost her inheritance during that same terrible year, they talked about the similarities of their lives and the problems they had known. But despite Armgard's best efforts, Ida grew weaker with each passing week.

Before long Anton was summoned, arriving just in time to see his mother before she died. He had not expected to be so hurt by her death; it left him not only motherless, but also guilty for not having seen more of her before she died. He blamed the war, his father, his lack of money, the Nazi regime and everything else he could think of. Edzard, too young to be aware of the relationships within his family, only remembers the macabre moment of being taken by his father to Ida's bedside to farewell her corpse.

After the funeral Anton, Armgard and Edzard returned to Berlin, where they heard rumours of Hitler's plans to invade Russia. Through his friends, Anton discovered that Germany was negotiating with Finland to allow troops into that country in order to launch an attack on their eastern neighbour. Armgard wondered how this would affect her parents, who were still living at the Norwegian Legation in Finland. Letters took a long time to reach her and she had no recent news. She knew that Finland had fought a terrible war against Russia the previous year, but it was only much later that she learnt the full story of the effect of the Winter War on the country itself and on her parents.

Before that war started, the Michelets' life in Finland had been trouble free and comfortable. The Finns enjoyed a good standard of living. Due to the huge agricultural lands in the east of the country, people were well fed and, although life in Helsinki lacked the luxuries and sophistication of pre-war Berlin, both Johan and Omi enjoyed their posting. However, on November 30th 1939, two months after the declaration of war, Russia invaded the east of Finland where the two countries shared a border. Although many Swedes and seven hundred Norwegians volunteered to fight for Finland, the governments of Sweden and Norway gave their neighbour no help other than a few armaments. Johan felt uncomfortable about this lack of neighbourly help, but did his best to explain to the Finnish press that his country, Norway, needed to keep its forces at home in case it should be attacked by the Germans – which indeed it was.

Despite being officially abandoned to their fate by their one-time allies, the Finns put up a spirited defence against the Russians. Knowing full well that Molotov and Stalin intended to push troops all the way through to Helsinki, they took every precaution possible. Some of the 'treasure of the country', Finnish children, were shipped to Stockholm. Everyone else, including Johan and Omi, existed on meagre rations, sparing as much food and fuel for the army as they could. Fearing what would happen if the Russians reached Helsinki, Omi sent her valuable Wilhelm Gentz paintings to Germany for safe keeping – a move she bitterly regretted when she heard they had been destroyed by Allied bombs.

The Winter War, as it was so chillingly called, was fought through snow and ice by determined, well-trained Finnish soldiers, dressed from head to toe in white. Though their numbers were small – infinitely smaller than their enemy – they had the advantage of being able to pick out with their guns the black–clad Russians as they moved westwards across the flat, snow–covered fields and frozen lakes. The Finns also invented – and used – the

'Molotov Cocktail' against Russian tanks. In the beginning these weapons were no more than a bottle filled with petrol or kerosene and a match taped to the side, but they were quickly improved by the addition of a sulphuric acid tablet at the bottom to ignite the fuel, and a small amount of tar to create smoke. Knowing how poorly the Russians maintained their vehicles, the Finns tossed their 'bombs' into the rear of the tanks where spare petrol was kept and the ensuing flames soon engulfed the greasy engines. In temperatures of minus 40 degrees, wounded Russians died quickly and those who tried to escape were shot.

In Berlin, Hitler watched the humiliation of Russia by the Finns and felt certain that quite soon he would be able to inflict the same damage on Russia himself. Meanwhile Stalin fumed over the massacre of his army and the incompetence of his officers, regretting that he had executed most of the well-educated army leaders. Quite soon he began the process of reinstating the few who were still alive.

In the snow-covered fields of eastern Finland, after three months of continuous fighting and more than 25,000 of their own soldiers dead, the Finns were running out of men and equipment. Their commander, Field Marshal Mannerheim, made a daring decision. He fired, all in one day, his last rounds of ammunition in the hope that the Russians would believe him capable of fighting on for a long time. He timed it well. The Red Army, which had already lost more than 100,000 soldiers in those three gruelling months, was becoming bogged down in the melting snow. Stalin offered a peace treaty, which Mannerheim accepted on 13th

March 1940, telling his people:

Peace has been concluded between Finland and Soviet Russia, a harsh peace in which Soviet Russia has been ceded nearly every battlefield on which you have shed your blood on behalf of everything we hold sacred and dear.

However, unlike Czechoslovakia or Poland, Finland remained independent in the wake of the Peace Treaty, though Mannerheim was forced to cede Finland's principal grain-producing area to Russia. Suddenly 40,000 Finnish refugees flooded into the west of the country, fleeing their homes in the surrendered lands rather than live under Russian domination. The Michelets, like everyone else, helped in any way they could, sharing what little they had and learning to live yet more frugally so that there would be enough food to go round.

It was hardly surprising that one year later the Finns announced they would allow Hitler to station troops in their country in order for Germany to attack Russia. The Allies, horrified that Finland was prepared to help their enemy, instantly withdrew all Embassy and Legation staff. Johan and Omi were transferred to Stockholm and were still packing when the first German troops arrived. Following in the footsteps of the troops came German administrators, bureaucrats – and journalists.

To the great relief of both Anton and Armgard, Anton was offered a job in Finland. *The Hamburger Fremdenblatt,* a newspaper for Germans overseas, asked him to remit articles about the progress of the war – always, of course, within the parameters set out by authorities in Berlin. He would, however, be away from the immediate arena of prying eyes and once again be able to travel around Europe for his work. Armgard was thrilled. Her husband would at last earn a salary with which to feed his family. Once they reached Finland, Edzard would soon recover from the coughing and wheezing that had beset him of recent months and the three of them would live far from the ever-growing propaganda and intimidation that seeped into every home, frightened all but the most staunch defenders of Hitler and smothered most forms of dissent in Germany.

As Anton set off from Berlin for Finland, he promised to call for his wife and son as soon as he received the permit for them to join him.

11

Wolfram Sievers' Offer 1941-42

During the autumn of 1941 Armgard struggled on in Berlin, stretching what little money Anton had left her when he set off for Finland. Somehow she made it last yet another month. And then another. Her weekly child allowance from the state was pitifully small; only mothers with four healthy children were well rewarded by Hitler's regime.

Each day she listened to news from Russia on the radio. Tante Sigrid's three sons were enlisted in the German Army and all played their part in the invasion, or *Unternehmen Barbarossa*, as it was proudly called by the government. Hitler was so determined his assault on the enemy would be a success that he chose one of his favourite pieces of music, the fanfare from the march finale of Liszt's *Les Prèludes*, to precede the victorious news each day. It seemed to Armgard that there would never be an end to this monotony of propaganda hiding in the music of Liszt.

When Anton left Berlin in July, one month after the start of Barbarossa, he led Armgard to believe that the permit to join him in Helsinki would come well before autumn set in. Now trees had shed their leaves and chill winter winds whistled through gaps in the windows of her rented room, Armgard patiently stuffed rags into the cracks and re-darned their clothes as she waited for his letter. In these last few months Edzard's coughing had become so frequent that she feared he would never stop. Sometimes she gathered him into her arms and rocked him gently to sleep, lying down beside him to lend him her warmth.

Edzard was now seven years old and, though thinner than ever, had nevertheless grown too tall for the few clothes he had. Neighbours were kind, passing on an old coat or a pair of mismatched socks for him to wear. She never confided to them that she hoped to be out of Germany soon, nor that she dreamt every day of living with her husband in Finland. They could so easily have misinterpreted her remarks as anti-Nazi and informed on her. She had learnt long ago that silence was her greatest ally.

Even when she visited Tante Sigrid she kept her longings to herself, not wanting to put her aunt under any suspicion. Tante Sigrid lived away from the centre of town and every room in her house was filled with lodgers. Yet when Armgard came to see her, she always delved into the back of a cupboard and managed to find an old jar of stewed apples or the stub of a coloured pencil

150

that had once belonged to one of her sons. Edzard beamed with pleasure at such a gift. Then later, over a cup of what passed for coffee, Tante Sigrid would admit to Armgard how much she feared for her own boys, all so young and all three of them now far away fighting the Russians. She knew the cause they fought for was right, but that did not stop her worrying day and night about them. Armgard comforted her as best she could.

When the eagerly awaited letter from Finland finally arrived it brought no joy. The permit was difficult to obtain, Anton wrote. He would be in touch soon.

She imagined his life in Helsinki. She knew the Finns had suffered terrible deprivations during the Winter War and that shortages of wheat and other food still existed. However, she also knew that conditions were considerably better than in Berlin. He had told her before he left that once he was in Finland he would be able to talk openly to foreign press representatives and that he would receive a press pass enabling him to travel to other countries in order to write articles for his newspaper. How she envied him that freedom.

And then she pictured her parents' life and the luxuries they enjoyed in Sweden – a neutral safe haven where food was readily available, doctors were on hand with prescriptions for sick children, and people could say anything they wanted without fear of being arrested. They could even listen to foreign radio broadcasts and read international newspapers. Sometimes she imagined her parents dining with other diplomats and conversing in a civilised manner about books or foreign travel – instead of always concentrating their minds, as she had to, on staying warm or searching the shops for an envelope in which to send a letter, or on the relentless, energy-sapping, all-encompassing daily search for food.

For Christmas, Armgard and Edzard managed to make their way to Stötterlingenburg. Both the big house, which her uncle Wolfgang von Lambrecht-Benda now occupied, and the older, smaller house in which Miriam was currently living, groaned with refugees. Despite the overcrowding and the damp winter air of the valley, Armgard relished the comforts of home and the glowing warmth of her grandmother's love.

Like most of the von Lambrecht-Bendas, Miriam still defended Hitler and even had a portrait of him in her house. As a Prussian and a loyal patriot, she felt sure that the Führer was doing his best for Germany and made up her mind to believe the propaganda she was fed daily on the radio. After all, she told Armgard, to oppose Hitler would be tantamount to supporting the enemy. Miriam had no wish to undermine either her own country or five of her grandsons who were fighting for the Fatherland in bitter campaigns.

At the end of January Armgard tore herself away and headed back to Berlin with her son, hoping to find another letter from Anton when she arrived. The train was overflowing. Passengers stood in corridors or sat on each other's laps. No one complained or even grumbled. Armgard wrote in one of her letters:

When I visited the toilet I found a soldier in uniform using it as a seat. He was too tired to move out. 'I'll sit on the floor while you use it', he told me. Life was governed by a new set of rules.

It was soon after her return from Stötterlingenburg that the first whispers of a circulating rumour reached Armgard's ears. Anton was well and still writing for the newspaper in Helsinki. But he was living with a lady. The lady in question - a Swedish-Finn - worked as a journalist. Anton had not obtained a permit for Armgard to join him because, as he eventually confessed, he no longer needed her. Armgard tried to imagine her rival: five years younger than herself, she would be pleasantly curved from eating enough food, whereas Armgard's skirts now hung loose around her. She had always been slim - 'too thin', her well padded mother and aunts used to complain - but in pre-war Berlin, when style counted for much, her friends constantly remarked on her elegance. Anton had been proud to escort her to parties in those days, showing her off to his friends.

'Have you ever seen such glorious hair?' he would ask them. 'I call it her auburn halo', and he would gently run the palm of his hand over the thick mane of shiny hair. Now that hair hung lank and lustreless around her shoulders. She seldom washed it; hot water was scarce.

On the other hand, Brita Gustafson - even the name of her rival upset Armgard - probably had shiny blonde hair that she could toss from side to side as she sipped a martini before dinner with her new lover. Despite an earlier marriage, Armgard learnt, Brita had no children; she was a journalist for United Press, the American news agency. It had always been Armgard's ambition to become a journalist and write for foreign papers; she had written a few articles before the war and her English was still fluent, but since Hitler's rise to power, women in Germany were discouraged from having careers. The Führer deemed they should consider themselves fulfilled by husband, children and home. Her longed-for career was stillborn.

And now she had been abandoned by her husband. Under other circumstances she might have allowed herself to wallow in self-pity for weeks on end, but even that luxury was denied. What little energy she still possessed must be spent on survival. She had to keep going for Edzard's sake. Since their winter visit to Miriam's cold house, his health had deteriorated yet further; sometimes he woke in the night with a forehead as hot as a furnace and by the morning his sheets were wet with sweat.

Before the war she had an excellent Jewish doctor, a friend of the family, but he had long since left Berlin. Now she waited her turn like everyone else until one of the surgeries offered her an appointment. A doctor examined the boy thoroughly then paused before giving his diagnosis: Edzard had tuberculosis.

Armgard sat motionless in her chair. Only her eyelids closed and then slowly opened again as she waited for him to offer some words of hope.

'I shall have to report his name to the authorities.'

She ignored that remark and asked instead how he intended to treat the disease. How could Edzard be cured?

The doctor made notes before looking up. Bland words came out of his mouth as if by rote – as if he had used them before. He told her that he could not treat Edzard, explaining that he had a wife and children and that he was therefore in no position to defy the rules. He was sorry ...

As he walked over to open the door for her, he murmured platitudes of goodwill and then, as she was leaving, confided to her that Germany once had famous sanatoriums, but now there were camps for all victims of tuberculosis. He urged her to keep her son away from the camps because they were not good.

Back at home, with Edzard tucked into bed, she pulled a blanket around herself and considered her options. On the day of her marriage to Anton she had given up her Norwegian passport. She did so willingly at the time; she had wanted so much to be his wife, to be a German like him. Now there was no way back. Not that Norway could have helped her. Although reports in the press suggested that occupied Norway was a happy country, she had enough friends in the resistance to know that was far from the case.

Her parents' comfortable life in Stockholm came once again to mind. She knew they lived in a flat provided by the Norwegian Foreign Office. Her mother would be happy if she and Edzard came to stay with them. It did not take much imagination to guess that her mother was overburdened by the guilt of her confused loyalties and that she probably needed Armgard as much as Armgard needed her. But she also knew that without a permit there was no way she, a German citizen, could leave the country. She would be caught and punished. Edzard would be taken from her. Even if, by a miracle, she managed to escape with her son, her absence would cause what was chillingly known as *sippenhaft*, (the liability of relations), the imprisonment – or worse – of family members. This was a warning from the Gestapo to dissuade people like herself from *abspringen* or 'jumping off'. Her grandmother had done nothing to deserve such punishment. Nor had Tante Sigrid or the Kuenzers.

Who could she turn to?

The Kuenzers had their own worries. Day by day they lived in fear of an authoritative knock on the door. Still involved with various opposition groups, Richard Kuenzer knew his life was in danger.

Tante Sigrid's hands were full enough coping with her many lodgers. She had no spare room for Armgard and Edzard. And Stötterlingenburg was not an option for them; Edzard's coughing always grew worse the moment he arrived in the damp valley of the Harz Mountains. There was no escape from the circle of hunger and struggle. No one in Berlin could help her. She was powerless and frightened.

I was writing down Armgard's memories of life at that time, as she told them to me, cross-checking with archives or history books to back up her account, asking her to repeat some parts or add more detail here and there. I kept the flow of her story in my mind even when I was far from my computer, ready to adjust and carry on as soon as I was back at my desk. But one day I received a phone call from Edzard that upset me deeply and changed everything I would write from then on. In 2003 I had flown back to the UK from Australia to spend Christmas with my son Magnus and his family in Suffolk. On Boxing Day we were totally absorbed watching games being played by my two small grandchildren – for once Germany and the war were far from my mind. Suddenly the phone rang. To my surprise, Edzard was on the line from Frankfurt.

'I had to ring Iain on the Isle of Skye to get Magnus's number', he said. 'I need to speak with you.'

'Is something wrong?' Though we now talked frequently, my cousin and I had never exchanged phone calls at Christmas.

'Yes, something is very wrong.' His voice suggested grim news. I waited, signalling to the grandchildren to make less noise, but it was Christmas after all and their spirits were high.

'It is not good.' He took a long deep breath, as if plucking up courage. 'My stepsister Maria and her daughter have been helping with our research about my father. She was going through some archives in Stockholm and she found a file on my mother.'

'Yes ...'. I filled in, wondering what could possibly have been upsetting about Armgard's file.

'It said she was an agent for the Nazis.'

As I stifled a gasp it was noticeable that even the children dropped their voices, no doubt struck by the look of horror on my face.

'That's not possible. She was never a Nazi in any way at all.'

'Maybe not. But she was an agent. I'll send you the file.'

Words of comfort and reassurance poured from my lips, but

157

nothing I said lifted his spirits. Edzard had spent the last ten years researching the story of his courageous uncle, Richard Kuenzer, a man who gave his life in a hopeless attempt to rid his country of the Nazis. Most of Edzard's German contemporaries would be loath to contemplate, let alone study, any of these subjects, yet he wanted to know the truth of what happened in Germany. But nothing, absolutely nothing, prepared him for this news about his mother.

There must be another side to the story. Somehow we'll find the truth, I assured him.

By then my mother had died. Not that she would have been any help, for in her declining years she allowed, even encouraged, her mind to lose touch with reality. On several occasions since my father's death, she had told me she only wanted to die in order to be with him once more. In the meanwhile sorrow, weariness of life – and whisky – all played a part in destroying her mind.

The day after my return to Australia I settled down at my desk to reread Armgard's own account of the next stage of her journey. I also checked events as she told them to me against the facts recorded in history books and began all over again to trawl archives in various countries – this time on a completely new line of enquiry. The fact that she became an agent was corroborated in other files and gradually a new story began to emerge.

I told a friend of mine, a novelist, about this research. 'Are you sure you want to carry on? Sometimes it is better for families not to know the truth. Sometimes the truth is too hurtful.'

But it was too late to stop now. Edzard knew the truth and

wanted the whole story. Now I must rewrite extensively. From this juncture onwards, I shall knit together Armgard's own vividly remembered account of her life in Berlin with the factual results of my latest research.

It must have been some time in the spring or summer of 1942 that Wolfram Sievers approached Armgard, changing her life forever.

Armgard knew, because her husband often recounted stories of his youth, that Wolfram Sievers and Anton had once been the closest of friends. While they were still in their teens, living near Stuttgart, the boys joined the *Wandervögel* – Wandering Birds – an organisation similar to the Boy Scouts. Camping under the stars, running races through fields and enjoying the freedom of being away from home for the first time, Wolfram and Anton forged a common bond.

In the early part of the 1920s, as Germany tottered on the brink of financial disaster, the *Wandervögel* began to take on a more political bias. Young lads were encouraged to turn their association into a patriotic group in which, around camp fires, they would sing the praises of their beleaguered country with songs such as '*Unsere Fahne flattert uns voran*' – 'Our flag leads us on'. It is hardly surprising that later, having brought prosperity and national pride back to Germany, Hitler was able to fold the *Wandervögel* into the Hitler Youth.

Anton's father strongly disapproved of Hitler from the very beginning; Armgard suspected that his father's disapproval egged his son on to listen with interest to the Chancellor's speeches. A year older than Anton, Wolfram was a born leader with an easygoing manner and a desire to help his country. He joined the Nazi Party and in time persuaded Anton to follow his lead. It was easy for young men to look up to a leader who seemed to have erased the shame of Versailles. Yet by 1933 Anton, then a journalist with some insight into what was happening in his country, began to distrust Hitler's motives and wanted to cancel his party membership, but warnings of reprisals and even imprisonment held him back from such a drastic step. Meanwhile Anton had introduced Wolfram to his sister, Madelaine. The pair soon became engaged. Though the marriage never took place, Wolfram remained on good terms with all the family.

In 1934 Wolfram Sievers attended Anton and Armgard's wedding wearing a swastika on his sleeve. At the formal dinner in Berlin's Grand Hotel he sat between his wife, Hella, and Armgard's Norwegian cousin, Harriet Michelet. Harriet remembered him as polite and friendly, though she said that even then the swastika made her uneasy.

After Anton and Armgard returned from their honeymoon, they invited Wolfram to dinner. He had a way of asking questions that endeared him to most of her other guests and he would have asked after Sisi, whom he had met at the wedding and whose husband was in the British Foreign Service.

Armgard must have known, because Anton would have told

her, that after joining the Nazi Party in the late twenties, Wolfram worked diligently and was soon picked out by its leaders as someone both able and articulate. He was well rewarded. Before long Himmler recognised his potential and promoted him to *Standartenführer* (Colonel) in the SS. The system sucked him into its elite branch until he found himself in a position of power over others, and the ladder that he had diligently climbed to achieve such a position had been removed from under him. There was no way out. His life was committed to serving Hitler. Reporting directly to Himmler, he had several duties, one of which was to recruit agents for Walter Schellenberg's AMT VI – the foreign political information service.

Through Himmler's network of spies, Wolfram kept a close eye on his friend Anton. He was aware that Anton was involved on the fringes of various illegal anti-Nazi groups. And of course Wolfram knew – it seemed everyone knew – that Anton had deserted his wife in order to live with his mistress in Helsinki.

When Wolfram approached Armgard he had an interesting proposition. The offer was tempting: she would be given a permit to take Edzard to a sanatorium in Arosa, high up in the healthy air of the Swiss mountains – not far from the German border.

There is no way of finding out how she came to a decision. Although almost everything in her life had crumbled around her, she was still quick witted and resourceful. She would have been aware from the onset that there were strings attached to this offer – maybe they were spelled out to her from the very beginning. If so, did she calculate that in time she would find a way to turn the tables and escape from the obligations that would be imposed on her? After all, for the first time in a long while she had been given a feeling of hope – and a chance to use her brain to her own and Edzard's advantage.

One thing is certain, because it is recorded in the files of public archives in both Sweden and Switzerland: she accepted Wolfram's offer. As summer was drawing to a close, Armgard and Edzard set off for Arosa.

12

The Cabinet War Rooms 1942-43

When Paddy reported for work at the Cabinet War Rooms in London, only ten days after returning from Shanghai, Sisi stayed on with his family in Scotland, together with her children and Peggy. Alongside many Noble cousins who were staying at Ardkinglas, as well as friends of the family from England and refugees from Belgium, she made herself useful by helping with chores. As she was always cold, the job of sawing logs appealed to her and she could be found outside for a couple of hours every day, wielding a large saw as she attacked yet another pile of fallen branches. The longer she stayed out of the house, the less time she had to listen to news on the radio or the discussion that followed it, whether it was praise for the Allied airmen who were bombing the hell out of Berlin or comments on the hateful behaviour of Germans.

No sooner had Sisi settled into her new life than Peggy announced she would leave her job as nurse to Iain and me for the duration of the war. She wanted to help her country and had applied to join the Women's Royal Navy, known as the WRENS; she was immediately accepted. During their months of internment by the Japanese, Peggy had become a friend to the family and Sisi felt a sense of abandonment now that both Paddy and Peggy had left her side.

By good fortune she found a new ally. Daisy Powell Jones had once been Sir John Noble's secretary; after his death she stayed on at Ardkinglas, where she was made as welcome as if she were one of the family. Some twenty years older than Sisi, Daisy took kindly to the withdrawn newcomer, inviting Sisi to her room to sit by the fire in the evenings while they darned a pile of clothes together and talked. In the shelter of Daisy's room, Sisi gradually unburdened some of her worst memories of their internment by the Japanese and then made Daisy chuckle merrily by describing their adventures with Darling in Africa. On days when rain came down so relentlessly that sawing logs proved impossible, she helped Daisy make butter. Daisy had taken on this task when rationing started; each day she poured milk fresh from the cows into wide bowls and left them in a cool part of the kitchen dedicated to dairy products. Later the cream was scooped off the surface and Daisy churned its thick liquid in a wooden vat until it turned to butter. Dividing the resulting solid into half-pound slabs, she marked the top of each with decorative diagonal lines and laid them on wooden plates. At mealtimes people helped themselves sparingly, for although it was delicious, there was never enough.

Each week Sisi received a letter from Paddy and rushed to Daisy's room to read her its contents. It gave her strength to know that with Daisy she could pour out her heart and through this friendship feel better equipped to cope with life in the Scottish Highlands.

Exhilarated by his new role in London, Paddy spared nothing of himself, saying later that the work he achieved during those years was the best of his whole career. He joined the Joint Intelligence Staff (JIS) three days after the outbreak of the Battle of Alamein. His job was to gather intelligence to share with the JIS in Churchill's underground Cabinet War Room. At eight thirty every morning he started reading inward telegrams at the Foreign Office, after which he consulted the Political Departments to get their views on any points that would be likely to arise at the next JIS meeting. Later in the morning he hurried round to the Cabinet War Rooms. He quickly worked out, down to the last yard, which was the shortest route between the two buildings. Marine sentries on guard knew all the regulars by sight, letting him weave past the sandbags and down into the bowels of the building without checking his identification.

Paddy had a desk in one of the rooms close to Churchill's own office; a wooden panel engraved with the names of the four occupants hung outside the door. When I first took my three children to visit the Cabinet War Rooms, soon after they were opened to the public in 1973, we were proud to see his name, *Sir Andrew Noble,* on one such panel. Unfortunately nearly all those panels, and the walls onto which they were attached, were removed during the huge renovations that took place between 1981 and 1983 to allow greater numbers of people to wander round what has now become a museum. Before those renovations the atmosphere was more intimate. Children under ten were not allowed to enter, but my younger son, five-year-old Patrick, was given special permission to join our tour on the grounds that his grandfather had worked in these rooms. He must have smiled endearingly, because he was allowed to sit on Churchill's hallowed chair while the guide explained to the rest of us the workings of the Cabinet War Rooms. The guide even placed one of the old man's hats on Patrick's auburn curls as he talked about Churchill's daily routine. We never thought to take a camera.

In 1942 the Joint Intelligence Staff consisted of five members, representing the Admiralty, the War Office, the Air Ministry, the Ministry of Economic Warfare and the Foreign Office. In his journal Paddy wrote:

I think we were a pretty efficient body and if we sometimes argued like mad round the table, it did not stop us from being good friends when we could get even a short distance away from our work, which wasn't all that often because the pressure was tremendous.

In her book, From the Inner Circle, A View of War at the Top, Joan Bright Astley described the atmosphere:

It was a strange life that we led in those days in our quiet dungeon galleries where the only mechanical sounds were the tap of typewriters and the hum of air-conditioning fans.

A notice board showed us if it was 'fine', 'wet' or windy outside, red or green lights if an air raid was 'on' or 'off'. If it was 'on' we heard nothing of it until we were outside the heavy steel doors of our cage. Then we would know by the frequency of the crump, boom or crackle whether or not it was worth going out into the normal blitz life of London. Long hours of work did not give anyone much opportunity for this anyway. The Planning and Intelligence Staffs lived on assumption, based their appreciations on likelihoods ahead of them. Daily truth belonged in the Map Room.

The Map Room lay next to Churchill's office and opposite the transatlantic telephone room where Churchill spoke on a scrambled line with Roosevelt. The basement offices were far from comfortable, but they afforded as much security for Churchill and his Cabinet as could be mustered at that time. There were rifles and gas masks to hand; thick walls and heavy steel doors with solid locking levers that would have probably delayed any seepage of gas or water – or invading soldiers. Paddy wrote:

Meetings of the JIS might continue until any hour. If we had not too much on hand I might get back to the Foreign Office by five thirty and home as early as eight. If on the contrary we had just handed down to us indirectly from Winston Churchill a paper with a horrible flag on it saying: 'Action this day', which for us almost always meant 'action this night', we might be at it till any hour. We were certainly there once until 5am. If we had to work after dinner, we usually dined in the War Cabinet

Offices, which put on remarkably good food under the circumstances; they had the only chef I knew during the war who could make good scrambled eggs out of dried eggs.

Paddy rented a top-storey flat in St James's Court, a short walk along the park from the Cabinet War Rooms. Accommodation at the top of a building was considerably cheaper because of the bombing, but Paddy thought it would make little difference whether he died at the top of a pile of ruins - or at the bottom. And anyway he was happy to pay the lower rent.

Paddy's journal went on:

On rare occasions when the departments could not reach agreement, we would finish with a joint meeting of the Joint Intelligence Sub-Committee and the JIS. This never failed to produce an agreed paper, though sometimes at the cost of dulling our opinions so as to meet the hesitations of one department, usually the War Office, who were inclined to say something like: 'We think the Germans will do this and that; but we cannot exclude the possibility they will do something quite different.' Churchill hated that.

Paddy worked long hours without breaks. When he was tired, one of his colleagues noted, he drew a cigarette from the silver case in his pocket, inserted it in a holder and inhaled slowly. Ashtrays were placed all round the room; most people used them at some time during the day.

The highlight of Paddy's work was 'Operation Overlord' - the invasion of Normandy. The first plan was put to the JIS at the end of July 1943, when they were asked to estimate the scale of German resistance in Western Europe between Holland and the Pyrenees on what would become 'D-Day', which it was then thought would be in May 1944. The JIS discussed the matter and replied that there was no way they could possibly guess that far ahead. But the planners insisted that if the JIS could not estimate what the Allies might have to fight, there was no way of knowing whether the operation was possible.

So Paddy and his team sat down to write a paper on the progress of the war over the coming months. Then they made an assumption of what they thought the Germans would do to resist the invasion and how the underground movements in France might operate. The lines of intelligence buzzed all over Europe and Paddy felt elated to know that he sat at the epicentre of a scheme devised to bring about the end of the war.

At Ardkinglas Sisi was beginning to feel that the war would never end. She had become, even in her own mind, a British citizen in every way, yet she sensed the other women were sometimes wary in her company. They all knew she had a German grandmother and a sister living in Berlin, so in retrospect their guarded behaviour was understandable, given the precarious nature of the intelligence work being carried out by members of the family and their house guests. As chatelaine of Ardkinglas, Elizabeth Noble coped stoically with the continuous and varied influx of family and friends who arrived, sometimes unannounced, to live in the house. Her husband, Johneen, Paddy's brother, spent much of his time working in Milton Keynes as a member of the select team hidden away at Bletchley Park, helping to penetrate German intelligence and eventually break their codes, while never letting slip to the outside world so much as a hint of what his work involved.

Guiton Floor and her two daughters, who were family friends of the Nobles from Belgium, had accepted hospitality at Ardkinglas. From 1940 until 1944 her husband Ides was working in the Belgian secret service, *La Sûreté de l'État*, to brief and organise resistance alongside the Special Operations Executive in Baker Street. In early 1944, at a time when preparing resistance networks for the Normandy landings was particularly vital work, there was a shortage of agents qualified to be parachuted into Belgium. So Ides, despite being well known to German counter-espionage services, insisted on going himself. His critical liaison mission accomplished, he made his way back to England via Gibraltar. He was awarded an MBE and DSO and many Belgian honours for what was later described as this 'gallant and spontaneous action'.

Although Sisi could not have known the roles being played by these men, she was well aware that her part-German background hung heavily in the air. So long as the war continued she knew she could never break through the invisible barrier that separated her from the other mothers.

Every morning my aunt Elizabeth mustered all the children staying in the house into what became known as 'the school room', where she gave us a basic education. Up to about twelve

Line up of children outside Ardkinglas in 1942, including Vanessa and
Stella Jebb, Sarah and Johnnie Noble and Iain and Laila Noble

children of mixed ages were taught by her at any one time: her
own children, Sarah and Johnny, Iain and myself, our cousins
Miles, Vanessa and Stella Jebb.

One day, while the children were busy in the schoolroom,
Sisi walked briskly up into the Argyllshire woods before starting
work with her saw. A gregarious person by nature, she had never
before walked anywhere on her own for pleasure, preferring the
company of friends or a game of tennis. But at this stage of her
life she found it calmed her mind to be away from the chatter
of the other women and the articles in the newspapers that they
discussed at length; naturally those with relatives in the army
watched the progress of the war with them in mind. Sisi needed
solitude for her own confused thoughts.

Only recently she had overheard at the dinner table that yet another German submarine had been dispatched to the bottom of the sea off the British coast, drowning all men on board. As she walked, she recalled the last news she had had from Armgard before she and Paddy left for Shanghai, telling her that her young cousin Hasso Stegeman, still only twenty years old, had been promoted to senior officer aboard a German submarine serving in the North Sea. The last time she had seen Hasso was at Tante Sigrid's house in Berlin, when his mother brought the shy young boy to meet Sisi just before Armgard's wedding. She wondered if Miriam had heard the same news, and what she was feeling at this point. How Sisi wished the Allies could quickly bring about the defeat of Hitler and allow this cruel war to end.

As she strode along the drive, Sisi's socks soaked up the damp through holes in her shoes. The two double sheets of brown paper she had inserted as a stop-gap proved inadequate. But suddenly the sun emerged from behind the hills, warming her bones and giving her strength. Even deep in the beech woods, shafts of sunlight shone through to illuminate pools of dark green beneath the trees and there, appearing through a cushion of moss, she noticed patches of small orangey-yellow mushrooms. She tore off her jacket, loading into it as many of them as she could, showing them proudly to the other wives on her return to the house.

Instead of congratulating her on her find, they reacted with horror. 'Those are toadstools, probably poisonous. Throw them away.'

'No, they're *Pfifferlinge*. They're good. I know them well. We used to pick them when I was a child in ... in the forest.'

'Don't expect us to try them.'

Defiantly she carried her jacket-load to the kitchen, where she cleaned and cooked her mushrooms. At the dinner table, to the amazement of the others, she ate them. The next evening she did the same. Despite the paucity of butter in which to fry them, they were the best food she had tasted since before her internment by the Japanese. Perhaps they evoked memories of happier days, when Miriam had cared for her so lovingly at Stötterlingenburg and Tante Sigrid had held their hands as she took Armgard and Sisi dancing off into the woods to collect *Pfifferlinge* for the family.

The following evening at dinner, Paddy's sister Tasia leant across her neighbour and announced to Sisi in a voice loud enough to be heard by many of those sitting around the table, 'I've checked the encyclopaedia. Those mushroomy things you were eating yesterday grow in France and they're called *chanterelles*. They aren't poisonous at all. If you pick a few more tomorrow, Sisi, I'd like to try some chanterelles with my dinner.'

Sisi smiled at her brave sister-in-law, resisting an urge to reach over and show her gratitude tangibly. Everyone at Ardkinglas was tired; the war had drained away their good humour and their patience. Little kindnesses meant much to her.

One day Johan Michelet turned up without any warning at Ardkinglas to visit his daughter. In his new role as a special envoy for Norway he was sometimes sent to London, flying in from Stockholm via Scotland – the only available route – on a British or American plane. On this particular trip he made a detour to spend a few days with his daughter and grandchildren, none of whom he had seen since before the war began. I was sitting in the schoolroom, trying to pretend I understood something Elizabeth was explaining about mathematics – or 'sums' as we called it – when we all looked up from our books to see my mother open the schoolroom door and usher in a man with a black moustache, so tall that his head seemed to scrape the top of the doorway. We watched silently as he strode up to one of the Smith daughters who was the same age as me, and addressed her in his funny foreign accent, 'My little Laila, how good to see you again'.

All the other children sniggered at the sinister man who didn't even know his own granddaughter, while I pretended to add up some numbers. Out of the corner of my eye I could see my mother dragging him towards me, causing my cheeks to burn bright red. How I wished they would just go away. That he was my grandfather did nothing to lessen my embarrassment. When eventually they left the room, my cousin Johnny announced in an all-knowing manner, 'That man is a German spy'.

I wished he had never come.

Only a few weeks after Johan's visit to Ardkinglas, Sisi received a letter from Rosemary, Paddy's older sister, inviting her to bring Iain and me south to stay with her in Surrey. Rosemary's husband was a Brigadier in the army; they had as yet no children of their own. She told Sisi that the house lay about an hour's drive from London and had plenty of room for the three of us.

Apart from a brief visit at Easter, Paddy had not been home to Ardkinglas. When he made the journey north again to fetch his family, he noticed how well Sisi looked. The exercise and fresh farm food had brought colour back to her cheeks and the weight she had lost during their internment in Shanghai was returning. He also noticed an expanding waistline. To her great joy she was able to give him the good news face to face: their third child was due in December.

Paddy brought his family south on trains so crowded that only elderly people or pregnant women found seats, but they were both too excited by the prospect of being nearer one another to care about the discomfort of the journey.

13

The Bombs that Fell on Berlin 1942-43

If only we had found out sooner about Wolfram Sievers' offer to Armgard, or if she had lived long enough to be able to explain her feelings about it, I could write now using her own words to describe the difficulties she faced. Unfortunately, soon after that Christmas when Edzard was given the shattering news, she was taken to hospital. Ninety-four years old, suddenly weak and unable to feed herself, she knew she was dying. Edzard caught a train from Frankfurt to hurry to her bedside. After checking she was well looked after and comfortable, he asked gently if it was true that she had been an agent during the war.

'Yes, it is true', she told him. 'But when I took you out of Germany, and later came out myself, no one was imprisoned or hurt on account of me – not like your father, whose family suffered terribly when he escaped to Sweden.'

She died soon afterwards.

When she told me, on one of my earlier visits to Basel, about taking Edzard to a sanatorium in Arosa during the war, I never thought to query how she had received permission to do so. She made it sound so plausible. Switzerland remained a neutral country and it was easy to assume she had been given some money by her grandmother, or sold another of her belongings, in order to fund the journey. I know now that when Armgard recounted her story about the war years from this point onwards she left out many details. How practised she had become at deflecting questions that were too near the mark, or throwing in enough interesting background information to steer my thoughts away from danger points. I wish for her sake she had felt able to discuss her work as an agent, to share her feelings and misgivings about it. But war is not solicitous of its victims; after the crushing defeat of Germany and all that the Nazi regime stood for, Armgard had little choice but to walk a long, lonely path of silence for nearly sixty years.

Sometimes Armgard and I studied books or newspaper cuttings together and that would lead to other subjects that interested her. Her mind never focused entirely on herself, but rather on the damage that war caused and the terrible tragedies she witnessed or heard about at first hand. But she could usually be brought gently back to the subject of her life, telling me how pleased she was that I kept notes about it. Of course she never mentioned Wolfram Sievers' name, or the assignment she accepted from him, but I believe that telling me about the hard times in Germany, though painful at first, gave her a certain measure of relief. Only now am I coming to understand why she was unable to divulge the one aspect of her life during the war that made sense of the whole story.

As it was, Edzard and I were left to rely on archives in many parts of the world for the bare facts of her role as an agent, and then it fell to me to merge them with Armgard's own stories as she told them to me.

When Wolfram Sievers offered Armgard the chance to take Edzard to a sanatorium in Arosa, he followed it up by introducing her to Dr Otto-Ernst Schüddekopf, head of an espionage department responsible for England and the United States.

It was Schüddekopf – known as PW in the spy ring – who enrolled Armgard in Amt V1, the department of *Sicherheitdienst*, (the intelligence service of the SS) that covered espionage in Western Europe. It is unlikely that Armgard did any work for Schüddekopf or his colleagues while she was in Arosa with Edzard; there is nothing noted in the records of any country's files – either at the time or after the war. Wolfram Sievers probably organised Edzard's stay in the sanatorium after hearing Armgard's account of her visit to the doctor. And of course it kept her and her son safe until her role as an agent could begin.

One thing is certain. By accepting his offer she sipped from a poisoned chalice. The tentacles of the SS spread far and wide. They had her covered now and she would have known it.

Armgard and Edzard left Arosa in January 1943. Once again homeless, she asked her father-in-law if they could stay for a while at his house in Stuttgart, which lay conveniently on her route back to Berlin.

Remseck, the Knyphausen family house, built on a hill above the town, was enveloped by carefully designed gardens extending up the hill to a spot dominated by the grave of Anton's grandmother. Although all the gardeners had left to fight the war, trees and shrubs still gave the gravestone and its surroundings an air of grandeur. Below the house, and stretching down towards the town, lay sloping fields that once yielded the owners a handsome income. The house itself was modest in size, despite being known as *Schloss Remseck* (Remseck Castle), yet it had many spare rooms since it was inhabited only by the seventy-seven-year-old widower Franz and his part-time housekeeper. Nevertheless, the door was firmly locked against outsiders who, he felt, might report on his illegal activity. Every afternoon he climbed the stairs and walked to one of the larger bedrooms where, having turned the key, pulled the curtains until they overlapped and placed a blanket across the bottom of the door, he switched on the radio to listen to the BBC German broadcasts. Franz hoped this crime would go unnoticed.

He was rash to take such a risk.

Franz's mother, whose gravestone on the hillside he erected after her death, was Jewish. Julia Mendez-Seixas was born and educated in New York, where her father served as Chief Rabbi for the Portuguese colony. It was in New York that she met and married Franz's father, Unico, who had come to America with the intention of fighting as a mercenary during the American Civil War. After their wedding the couple continued to live in New York, where Franz was born, before deciding to settle in Switzerland.

Franz inherited Remseck from a childless couple in the 1920s. By 1938, as the Nazi witch-hunt for people with Jewish blood intensified, the Stuttgart police had marked his records with a J for Jude, although he was not a practicing Jew. Franz knew that tuning in to the BBC put his life in danger, even without his Jewish connection. According to the law of September 1939, listening to any foreign broadcasts, including those from neutral countries, was forbidden. Over the ensuing years, 'Wireless Supervisors' were appointed to report on anyone breaking the rules. Yet, the BBC German service, now under the stewardship of Hugh Carleton Greene, Anton's friend, still attracted a small but steady audience, despite the increasingly savage penalties imposed on those who were caught. Perhaps the excitement of the risk he was taking filled a void in Franz's life or covered other pains.

He had become a recluse and was not welcoming when Armgard asked him for a temporary roof over their head for herself and Edzard. He disliked children and had little time for Armgard. He probably carried a sense of guilt because his son

Anton with his Jewish
grandmother Julia

had abandoned her or maybe, for one reason or another, his self–
esteem had shrivelled away along with his bank balance, so that
he no longer cared about anyone but himself. Looking out of the
window as he addressed her, he suggested that Armgard and his
grandson lodge each week in a *pension* in Stuttgart, but during
weekends, he said, they could live with him. Edzard remembers
being taken with his mother to listen to those BBC broadcasts
during the weekends they spent with his grandfather. 'I can still
remember the sound of bells ringing first and then a voice saying

"This is BBC London calling".'

The *pension* where Armgard and Edzard shared a room during the week was filled with an eclectic group of displaced Germans, most of whom, for one reason or another, were loath to discuss the real reason for their presence in that drab lodging house.

Armgard was happy to keep her thoughts to herself. The archives tell us that as an incentive to join the *Sicherheitdienst* she was offered a job teaching at the German Academy in Stockholm after her return from the clinic in Arosa. It is possible that she waited in Stuttgart, which she deemed safer than Berlin, hoping to hear that the job was hers. She must have looked forward to teaching, knowing that it would satisfy her craving to use her mind usefully. Above all, she yearned to get out of Germany.

The weeks dragged by. Each day she took Edzard to school, standing in queues for food until it was time to fetch him again. A memory from those schooldays is still vivid in Edzard's mind. Every day when the teacher walked into their classroom, the children were told to stand, raise their right arm upwards and intone '*Heil Hitler*'. One morning in early February, as soon as the class sat down after their salutation to the Führer, the teacher told them to pay attention while she described the fall of Stalingrad. The German Sixth Army, after four months of icy weather and virtual starvation, had lost 400,000 soldiers and finally surrendered. On the blackboard the teacher drew a circle to depict the town surrounded by Russian troops. Then slowly a smaller circle was drawn inside it and another - until it only resembled, to Edzard's eye, a target for shooting practice. For weeks afterwards he turned the image over and over in his mind, trying to work out the significance of it all.

A few days later the first British bombs started to fall on Stuttgart. Sirens wailed all over town and, leaning out of the window, Armgard could see a low-flying plane firing machine guns into the street. She lost no time in grabbing Edzard and rushing down to the basement, where they found their fellow lodgers sitting on wooden chairs or benches. They all had at their feet a suitcase packed with money, passport, jewellery and any documents they would require in the event of a hasty escape from the building.

Edzard remembers trying to sleep in the basement but being disturbed constantly by the walls shaking as yet more bombs landed closer and closer to them. Dust and the stench of fear filled the crowded space. Lights went out and he started to cough again. After a while fire engines wailed outside, followed by another series of detonating bombs. Some hours later the all-clear sirens sounded, allowing them to climb onto the roof for some fresh air and to peer through the smoke at the damage inflicted by Allied bombs. Since the *pension* was situated on a hill overlooking the valley of Stuttgart, he watched in fascination and horror as fires burnt throughout the entire city. He remembers that one evening an official walked up to his mother and pointed at him. 'Take this child down to his room. He is not allowed up here.'

Edzard and his school friends soon invented a new game. Each morning as they walked to school they collected shards from exploded shells and stuffed them in their rucksacks. The variety of shapes and sizes gave hours of satisfaction and discussion, as well as all the fun of swapping treasures.

By early March, unable to find enough food during the week in Stuttgart to feed herself and Edzard, Armgard headed back to Berlin. She packed their belongings and walked with Edzard to the railway station, carrying their suitcases. People crowded the building, juggling for position, searching for the correct platform because, since signboards no longer existed, everyone had difficulty knowing which train to board. Armgard and Edzard sat on a train they thought was bound for Berlin, only to be told that the Berlin express had just puffed out of sight on the other side of the platform. For a whole day they wandered the streets, cold and hungry, longing for the hours to pass until they could board the evening train. It was a slow journey through the night, stopping at every station along the way. At first light they awoke to voices shouting at them to collect their belongings and get off the train. They were at a station in an outer suburb of Berlin. The passengers started whispering to each other as they huddled in groups, trying to discover what was happening. Eventually Armgard learnt that a bomb had destroyed the main station in Berlin that very day, just as the earlier express train from Stuttgart arrived, killing many people at the station and on the incoming train. Too tired to speculate on the hand of fate that saved their lives, they boarded one bus after another, taking them towards the centre of Berlin until they arrived, exhausted, at the Kuenzers' house.

It must have been while they were lodging with Richard

and Gerda that Schüddekopff of the *Sicherheitsdienst* approached Armgard again. He was not yet able to arrange a job for her to teach at the German Academy in Stockholm, but offered her a permit to take Edzard to Sweden, with the proviso that she must come back to Berlin when she had safely delivered him. He probably reminded her about *sippenhaft*, the law whereby members of a family could be arrested and imprisoned for the misdeeds of a relative. She had no heart to be the cause of her grandmother's incarceration – and possible torture – in a Nazi prison.

Armgard once more packed their few belongings, and left for Sweden. They caught a train to Copenhagen, where Edzard was given an egg for breakfast, followed by sugared buns and a mug of hot chocolate. He thought he had arrived in paradise. His mother dragged him away to catch a ferry across the water to Malmö and from there a train to Stockholm. Somehow they found their way to her parents' flat and the enveloping arms of Omi.

After enjoying the luxury of her mother's care for two weeks, Armgard had no alternative but to make the move back to Berlin; had she stayed in Stockholm, not only would her grandmother and Tante Sigrid have been arrested, but she and Edzard would also have been in grave danger. There were more than enough German agents in Sweden to ensure that her treachery would be punished. Reluctantly leaving Edzard in her mother's safekeeping, she returned to Berlin, where she rented a room and found work as a typist and translator while she waited for the call that would signal that she could return to Stockholm to teach at the German Academy.

Armgard's employers in Berlin were I.G. Farben, a company that contributed financial support to Hitler and had links in the earlier part of the war to American chemical businesses. One of the I.G. Farben offices in Berlin, known as NW7, was later said to have been a key Nazi overseas espionage centre. Armgard's job was to translate documents into English, but there is no record to show in which branch she worked. Whether she was introduced by Wolfram Sievers or Schüddekopff, or whether she found the job on her own, we shall never know. I.G. Farben, at locations outside Berlin, was engaged in grim enterprises: one of their companies produced Zyklon B – a gas used in concentration camps.

Armgard knew nothing of this. Many years later she wrote to me proudly about her work as a translator at Farben. Had she had known of their work on the production of gas, she would have omitted from her later recollections the name of her employers. She simply wrote about the relief of finding a job and added that though her salary was low, it covered the rent of a room. Working with women who were stenographers, typists and telephone operators – and two elderly men – she concentrated on her translations and only occasionally stopped to chatter with her colleagues. They would discuss where to barter some tea for an egg or how to unpick and reknit a child's sweater that had become too small. No one asked questions because everyone had aspects of their life they preferred not to divulge. Yet the comradeship was nevertheless palpable.

'I lived in a city where you couldn't get hold of an envelope or toilet paper, a toothbrush, candle or pencil, and where everything that was broken had to be mended at home, yet you couldn't buy glue, nails or string. Even coffins were virtually unobtainable. But the greatest problem was hunger. It wasn't the kind of hunger when you think you are ready for the next meal. It was a continual gnawing ache reaching out to every corner of your body until you could think of nothing other than food. Yet you didn't dare let those feelings take over or you would have been done for. You just had to learn to ignore your body and concentrate on other things. Some people couldn't do that. They died from minor illnesses because they got too weak to combat the disease. There was only one consolation. In the midst of all that: people were so helpful to one another. Work colleagues and neighbours, we all did small things to help one another.'

The bombs had been falling sporadically on Berlin for some time, but on 23rd August 1943 Sir Arthur (Bomber) Harris returned to his 'area bombing' technique and tackled Berlin. Berliners called it 'terror bombing'. That first night seven hundred and twenty-seven British RAF planes unloaded nearly two thousand tons of bombs on the city, leaving a blanket of smoke next morning that smothered the city for days. Forty of those bombers failed to return to base, but the air raids continued. Harris planned to destroy Berlin from end to end, creating such chaos that German surrender would be inevitable.

He miscalculated.

On that first night alone, nearly six thousand Berliners died. Yet the destruction, far from demoralising the inhabitants, bound them together in common suffering and rallied them defiantly round the Nazis. Under those conditions, loyalty to the Fatherland was almost the only comfort available to the women, children and elderly men who huddled in the air raid shelters day after day and night after night.

In London, intelligence lines of contact were running hot on the topic of the bombing. Their concern was not for civilians but for the effectiveness of their actions to bring about an end to the war.

One message to the Foreign Office on September 7th 1943, from Arthur Yencken, an Australian serving at the British Embassy in Madrid, stated:

To judge by a number of despatches from Berlin, the Germans are in high spirits in technical circles at least about the RAF bombardments as they think they have found an antidote to bombing Berlin by the employment of night fighters ... a captured British pilot declared that the [latest] attack had been completely broken up by German night fighters, which heavily outnumbered the bombers.

A reply to Yencken can be found in the Foreign Office files at the Public Records Office in London, and is reproduced on the next page. Hand-written on September 10th 1943 by Paddy Noble in his instantly recognisable script, it starts:

As a matter of fact, the last raid on Berlin on 3rd of September was, I understand, particularly successful. The raid on the first was not one of our best ...

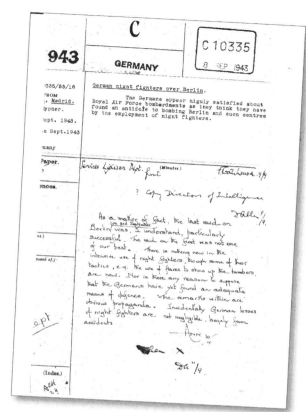

Foreign Office Memo September 1943, showing Paddy Noble's handwritten comments: 'As a matter of fact, the last raid on Berlin on 3rd of September was ... particularly successful.'

Did he think of Armgard as he considered the bombing of Berlin?

Armgard dreaded the air raid sirens. Each time they sounded she rushed to open her windows; left closed, they would have been instantly shattered by exploding bombs, and replacing window-panes was a costly business. In the early days of bombing, a little coffee or wine could be used as barter. But as the bombing continued, the glaziers demanded ever-higher prices. When one of her panes shattered, and this sometimes occurred even if the windows were left open, she made her way to the store rooms where her furniture was locked away and returned with a piece of silver or a rug. But Armgard knew that once the new glass was installed and paid for, she would still be at the mercy of bombs the following night, when the whole building might be destroyed.

Every afternoon, when the siren started, she ran home from work, opened her windows and moved quickly down to the shelter, where she waited, sometimes for several hours, until the all clear sounded. Then she joined other women throwing buckets of water to stop the raging fires. Buckets passed from hand to hand. Sometimes water ran out. Often the streets themselves blazed with phosphorus - the burning, seething result of incendiary bombs. Later, at about ten o'clock at night, the siren would break through the dark stillness, followed by the spine-chilling roar of yet more bombers overhead. At this point, day after day and night after night, the whole ritual started again. Luckily most Berlin flats were solidly built and the generous width of the streets was an important factor in keeping the fires under control. Beneath every block of flats lay a basement that was now used as a shelter. Holes had been cut through from one basement to another - sometimes the length of a whole street. Thus, as one building received a hit, the inhabitants crawled through to the next.

Not far from the centre of Berlin was the house where the painter Wilhelm Gentz, Armgard and Sisi's great-grandfather, had lived. In this oriental-style house his paintings depicting the Ottoman Empire and most of his archival material was kept. In 1943 a bomb fell on the building and the ensuing fire destroyed every painting.

Sometimes Armgard travelled by *U-bahn* to spend the weekend with Tante Sigrid, crowding in with her many lodgers and other homeless people. Sigrid and her husband Paul Stegemann lived in a house in one of Berlin's outer suburbs – now he had reached fifty-eight years of age, he was considered too old for active service. All three of their sons were still fighting Hitler's war against the Russians.

On a grey autumn day they received the terrible news that one of their sons, Harald, had been killed in action. Fifty-five years later his brother Bolko wrote to me:

Yes, we are identical twins. I heard about his death when I was fighting in Russia. It was terrible news and I remember feeling emotional minutes which just now in writing come up again. These emotions could fill a book. When I met my parents in 1944 on leave for some days, we did not talk about that. I had to go back to Russia.

Tante Sigrid now worried ceaselessly about her two remaining sons. The news on the radio was still positive – even optimistic of victory. Armgard, who learnt the truth on her visit to Stockholm, had no heart to tell her aunt that Germany was by now suffering an ignominious defeat at the hands of the Russian winter and the Red Army.

Although sentiments disloyal to the Nazi regime were being voiced by a few brave people in tightly protected circles, hidden behind closed doors where a password was needed before entry, most Germans remained true to Hitler. Tante Sigrid was one of them. Only a year after Harald's death, their eldest son Jürgen was killed in Poland. She had lost two sons fighting for the Fatherland and she was left with no option but to grasp the only consolation available to her: the knowledge that they were heroes. If the Führer were seen in a new light as having made mistakes or, worse still, as having betrayed his country, she would have lost her sons for nothing. She could not accept such heartache, preferring instead to continue supporting Hitler and his war – for better or worse.

Most shops in Berlin had closed down, but a few necessary services carried on. Dentists were a drain on resources; when Armgard needed a filling to cure a painful toothache, she was expected to hand over a gold ring to be melted down so that part of it could be used for the filling. No alternative existed and many people coped stoically with raging toothache in order to preserve the little barter they had. On the other hand hairdressers, provided the building in which they operated had not been *ausgebombt* by the Allies, were still open for business – and even affordable. Now that she was receiving a salary, albeit a small one, Armgard sometimes indulged in the luxury of a visit to the hairdresser, taking her own towel. Beer was used as a shampoo, since there was no soap. Somehow beer was always obtainable, whereas soap had become a commodity almost as valuable as food. Every once in a while it was possible to obtain a tiny piece with a coupon, but mostly Armgard learnt to do without.

Feechen, her young aunt in whose schoolroom at Stötterlingenburg she and Sisi had first been educated, returned to Berlin at this time, from Prague. She complained to Armgard about the stench that pervaded underground shelters, hallways, public transport and shops. Armgard explained that since they were only allowed a little warm water once a week, and must use it both for themselves and their clothes, it was hardly surprising that people emanated a foul smell. And anyway, she told Feechen, after a while you just learnt to ignore the smell – and many of life's other difficulties – otherwise it would have been impossible to keep going.

On 18 November 1943, Allied bombing started again. The so-called Battle of Berlin was relentless. On November 24th alone, eight to ten thousand people were killed and the following day the city resembled a sea of flames.

Goebbels wrote in his diary: '*Hell itself seems to have broken over us.*'

Chaos ruled in Berlin. Many of the central administrative offices went up in flames. The building that housed the department of I.G. Farben where Armgard worked received a direct hit and her job collapsed along with the building. Without a job she had no money for rent. As if that was not enough of a problem, a letter arrived from her mother in Sweden explaining that Edzard had broken his arm; he was in plaster and very uncomfortable. The letter finished with news that disturbed her even more. Omi ended her letter by admitting that Edzard often came home from school in tears because the Swedes had become very anti-German.

When Schüddekopff approached Armgard again, she was eager to listen. He still had not been able to get her a job at the Germany Academy in Stockholm as originally suggested.

However, he gave her a permit to leave Berlin for Sweden, where he knew she would be able to live with her parents and once more be classed as the daughter of a Norwegian diplomat. When she reached Stockholm, her duty would be to attend as many diplomatic and other social events as possible and report back to him the latest political and social gossip. The city was known to be full of international spies and some of them let slip morsels of information at diplomatic gatherings, where they felt they were among friends.

And another thing. He wanted information regarding her brother-in-law – called Noble – in London.

Her permit to leave Germany was granted by Walter Schellenberg, head of *Siecherheitsdienst Amt V1*, the foreign arm of Himmler's SS. Members of her family would not be arrested as she left Germany, or for as long as she continued to hand in reports.

Before leaving Berlin, Armgard spent a few nights with Gerda and Richard Kuenzer. In a letter she wrote to me fifty years later, Armgard told this story:

The IG Farben offices where I worked had been bombed and the Government Offices which housed all my papers had gone up in smoke, therefore the authorities had no way of tracing me. So I took the opportunity to leave for Sweden where I joined Edzard who was sick, and my parents.

She probably explained her departure to the Kuenzers with the same words. They must have believed her because Gerda and Armgard remained friends after the war, continuing to visit each other right up until the time of Gerda's death.

Richard Kuenzer wished Armgard well on her journey to Sweden and explained that he was trying to find new ways to communicate with members of the opposition who had escaped abroad. He was still involved in various underground meetings where they discussed intricate peace plans they intended to put into place after the overthrow of Hitler. These involved politics, economics and international diplomacy in order to restore Germany to its rightful place in the civilised world. The meetings were by now held as seldom as possible, with a minimum of participants, as large groups drew unwanted attention. Richard knew all too well that every person on the street could be a potential informer, that many phone lines were tapped and every suspicious act taken as proof of guilt. Anyone overheard using a phrase that even mildly questioned the Nazi regime was labelled a *Volks Verhetzung* – and punished. Yet Richard was unwilling to stand by while yet more atrocities took place, and was still prepared to risk his own life to get rid of Hitler. He asked Armgard to carry a letter to Sweden for him.

On the evening before her departure, behind closed doors in the deep of night, Richard and one of his friends discussed ways to achieve a democratic Germany, including the assassination of Hitler. They told Armgard that a number of German political refugees in Sweden had formed themselves into a group, working to persuade either Churchill or the Americans to give support to the opposition. They needed both undetectable explosives and a guarantee for the post–war settlement. As he began to talk she found a blanket and wrapped it firmly around his radio.

'You must be more careful', she warned him. 'There are microphones everywhere. The first place they put them is in a radio'.

She also suggested they were laying themselves open to horrendous retribution by the Nazis without any hope of success. 'Roosevelt wants *nothing less than unconditional surrender*. Why would the Americans, or their allies, change their mind?'

Knowing that Richard and his friends would carry on their work regardless of such warnings, she could only admire their courage and offer to carry Richard's letter.

What neither Richard nor Armgard understood, what they had no way of understanding, was that the Allies no longer saw a distinction between a decent patriot and the brutal Nazi. They were both German. The Allies distrusted all Germans.

And what neither of them knew, and had no way of finding out, was that some of the senior Nazis, aware by now that Germany might soon be defeated, had begun furtively to find a way of achieving an honourable peace with the Allies. Which of the people Armgard would be working for were leading double lives? There was no way of knowing. The world she was about to enter was one so full of secrets, lies and dangerous intrigue that her safety would depend on the sharpness of her brain and her ability to act the part of an innocent diplomat's daughter to perfection.

But for the time being there was only one thought on her mind. In a few days, she would be able once more to hug and comfort her son.

14

The Normandy Landings 1944

During the month of May 1944, no matter how hard the organisers tried to camouflage the fact, residents of villages all over the south of England became aware of more motorised movement than usual. In Surrey, gossiping villagers started spreading wild rumours. The postmistress told Paddy's sister Rosemary that her friend had seen long lines of military convoys heading south. Speculation was rife and wild assumptions were whispered from one person to another. There was a nervous fear as women listened to news on the radio more frequently than ever. Were the Germans about to invade or was the British Army setting off to rescue France? Someone had seen a truckload of sombre young recruits; maybe they were building a new training base nearby? Nobody knew and everyone had an opinion. The daily news bulletin on the radio remained obstinately silent on the matter.

One morning while I was at school, Sisi washed a pile of clothes. She heaped the wet garments into a basket and carried them to the garden, allowing the first rays of summer sun to warm her back as she hung them on a clothesline that stretched from one apple tree to another. Wandering back into the kitchen, she became aware that Rosemary was talking to someone. Guessing quite rightly that it was the pensioner who had offered to bring them an onion from his vegetable garden, she was about to walk in and introduce herself when she realised they were talking about her.

'But she isn't British is she?'

'She most certainly is', answered Rosemary without hesitation.

Sisi stood silently in the kitchen, unable to walk away in case they heard her footsteps and yet hating herself for remaining hidden behind the door while they discussed her.

Rosemary's voice continued. 'She's had a British passport since marrying my brother, and her three children are British through and through. So you see she now has roots here in Britain, not only through my family, who love her dearly, but through her children. And the roots through her children, if you just stop and think about it, are the most binding ties of all.'

There was a pause while he digested the information. But he needed further reassurance. 'There's something … I mean …

where exactly was she born? It's just that people are talking you see. There are rumours that ...'

'You tell your inquisitive friends that she was born in Norway. A country cruelly occupied by the Nazis. Her father's name is Michelet because his family originally came to Norway from France. Another country occupied by German troops. Sisi has good reason to keep herself to herself. She's as nervous and worried as you and I.'

On the 23rd December of the previous year, Sisi had given birth to her third child, my brother Timothy, known as Tim from the start. While Sisi remained in hospital after her confinement near Rosemary's home in Surrey, Paddy worked throughout Christmas in the Cabinet War Rooms. A skeleton staff kept the offices running smoothly, all of them cheerful under the circumstances, hoping that the secret work they were doing would soon bring about a German surrender.

Although Sisi spoke English without an accent, from time to time she used a phrase in an un-English fashion or mispronounced the name of an English town. To her children, however, she sounded just like everyone else. In the late afternoons, when we returned from school and it was too dark to play outdoors, she would read Kipling's poems to us until we knew every word of 'The Elephant's Child' by heart and loved echoing her words: 'the great grey-green greasy Limpopo River all set about with fever trees'. She represented continuity and security; she was home and hearth and love and comfort, neither losing her temper nor ever raising her voice when she admonished us, no matter how grave our misdemeanour. And if she sometimes appeared reserved, or slow to heap words of love on us – or praise for our achievements – we accepted that as normal.

While she waited impatiently for Paddy's weekend visits, Sisi busied herself by helping Rosemary clean the house, as well as joining in household jobs, which included endless darning of clothes, heating up leftover bits of soap to form them with the hands into a useable piece, and taking ration books down to the village shop, where there was always a long queue for basic items of food. The compassion Rosemary felt for her sister-in-law was unspoken. They discussed the weather and how they could concoct a nourishing soup from some left-over turnips and one potato; onions were hard to come by. They never talked about Germany.

In January, Iain was sent to Summerfields, a boarding school at which Paddy had once been a pupil. I still attended the local school in the next village. Each morning Sisi left Tim in Rosemary's charge and walked through the woods with me to the spot where a group of other mothers waited for a retired farmer to pick us up and drive us to school in his farm vehicle. In later years my mother told me how awkward she felt when she joined the other mothers. She sensed that as she approached they seemed relaxed, leaning inwards to throw tit-bits of gossip from one to another while they waited. But when she was among them they stiffened and moved apart, allowing space for her to join them and for their intimacy to seep away.

Sometimes the children taunted me. 'Your mother's not

British, is she?'

'Yes she is. Well, she's a little bit Norwegian, I s'pose.'

But without even waiting for my answer, they held up guns fashioned out of sticks and started shooting into the air as they chanted:

> *Hun, hun, evil hun,*
> *We will kill them every one.*

I had no idea what it was all about, but I never liked those boys.

Paddy's weekend visits were all too short. Sometimes Rosemary would tactfully arrange to have supper with neighbours on the Saturday night, so Paddy and Sisi could be alone for a few hours, holding hands and sipping some rather ordinary wine that Paddy managed to bring down from London.

Sisi, curling even more deeply into herself, already had a sense of foreboding, fearing that she might somehow lose Paddy on account of her German relations. She would do everything in her power to prevent that happening.

Paddy made the most of these brief escapes from work, relaxing by playing games with Iain and me or performing well-rehearsed acts of magic with his handkerchief, which enthralled us time and time again. However, it always seemed to him that he had barely more than a few hours with his family before departing again on Sunday evening.

In February 1944 Paddy had taken part in a high-level conference presided over by Air Chief Marshal Sir C.F.A. Portal, and attended by General D.D. Eisenhower and General C.A. Spaatz of the Eighth Army Air Force. Among the British contingent were Air Marshal Sir A.W. Tedder, Air Marshal Sir A.T. ('Bomber') Harris and Air Marshal Sir T. Leigh-Mallory. At the bottom end of the table were Kennedy and McMullen from the War Office, Lawrence from the Ministry of Economic Warfare, and Paddy himself, representing the Foreign Office. They were planning Operation Overlord, a top-secret invasion that would become known in later years as the Normandy Landings or D-Day.

The details involved in the landings required not only secrecy and careful teamwork, but also hours of collecting and collating intelligence from all over Europe. They discussed the bombing of German oil refineries, French marshalling yards and the bridges around the battle area and were also responsible for organising a sophisticated programme of deception to mislead the Germans. Paddy, not normally an early riser, was so engrossed in the project that he enjoyed leaving his bed early every morning to get started on the day's work. He was part of a team, and Operation Overload would, he was convinced, hasten an end to the war.

Now in the Cabinet War Rooms and all over the south of England the results of many months of intelligence work were at last coming to fruition. By the beginning of June, Paddy was full of apprehension. His days at work grew longer and his nights were often sleepless; he would lie in bed turning every detail over and over in his mind, hoping that his team had covered every eventuality. They had devoted a vast amount of effort and ingenuity into convincing the Germans that the Allies would invade elsewhere and at a different time. Paddy guarded every word he spoke, so as not to give away the slightest clue. Even weather reports were hush-hush in case something was unintentionally leaked about the date of the landing.

As the invasion commander, Eisenhower had chosen June 5th for D-Day, after taking advice from experts on the weather and on the exact movement of tides. However, despite the forecasts, bad weather set in on June 4th and a nerve-wracking delay of twenty-four hours was ordered. Finally, in the middle of the night of June 5th, the first aeroplanes took off, followed by an early-morning landing on the beaches of Normandy and a continuous barrage of bombs destined to fend off the Germans. Paddy wrote:

I can remember quite clearly standing on the balcony of my flat in St James's Court and watching the bombers go out for the first strike against the Normandy defences. I knew the landing was going in and it happened that the radio at the moment was playing a song of Vera Lynn's called 'There'll be Bluebirds over the White Cliffs of Dover'. The conditions were not too good and I went to bed with much anxiety. I went round to the Cabinet War Offices earlyish in the morning to hear that the initial landing had gone well, though the Americans were having a tough time on Omaha Beach. When I heard Eisenhower broadcast to announce the landing was in progress, I said to myself, 'Well, thank God that's a secret I no longer have to keep'.

I can't tell you what our work in the JIS was about. Some of the secrets have not yet been disclosed, and perhaps never will be.

By now the people of London were exhausted, but there was no respite. A new threat tested them to the full. Hitler was sending over his latest weapon, the flying bomb, and aiming it at

London. As soon as the bombs became a threat, Londoners gave them a comical name as a way of dealing with their own fear. The pilotless planes became known as *doodlebugs*. Paddy lay in bed on the top floor of his building and listened to their approach, which sounded not unlike a large motorcycle. At some point the vibration of the pulse motor would set up a sympathetic vibration that rattled windows, and at that point he knew the doodlebug was uncomfortably close. If the engine stopped, he wrapped a pillow round his head to protect it from flying glass and hoped the wretched thing would not land on his building.

The doodlebugs killed thousands, and those who did not die were crushed under falling masonry or seriously injured by broken glass. In Surrey, Rosemary and Sisi were terrified by a doodlebug that passed low over Farnham and landed in woods not far from the house. Fortunately it only created a large untidy hole and failed to damage either people or properties.

But it was evident that though the Normandy Landings had been a large step forward, they had not brought an end to the war.

One morning later that year, Sisi drew me from the breakfast table as she did every school morning and, picking up my satchel from the hall bench, led me out of Aunt Rosemary's house. Together we hurried along the short cut through the woods until we reached the clearing where mothers and children gathered to wait for the school transport. As soon as the farmer arrived with his ancient vehicle, all of us children clambered on board, waving to our mothers and holding tight to the rickety sides – or to each other – as he drove off. On this particular morning the farmer had barely turned the first corner when one of the schoolgirls called out to him, begging him to stop. She told him she had left her schoolbook on the ground while we were waiting for him. The farmer, surprised by this sudden change from his routine, eased his vehicle to a standstill and peered round at the girl.

'Don't think I'm going to turn around now. There's a war on you know, and petrol's hard to come by. But I'll give you five minutes to run there and back. Take that new girl with you to help you find it. Now hurry.'

She grabbed me by the hand and we ran as fast as we could back to the clearing. While the girl searched for the book, I saw someone moving through the trees. It was my mother collecting firewood on her way back to the house. I watched as she bent down to add another branch to her armful and then quite suddenly she stood up straight with a puzzled expression on her face. She had been startled by the sound of footsteps crashing through the undergrowth and now she peered at an approaching man.

He called out her name, 'Sisi'.

She must have recognised him because she took a step backwards. And then another. She looked from left to right like a cornered deer, but he kept coming and as he closed in, he tried in an awkward fashion to put his arms around her. She pushed him away, using her armful of branches as a shield between them. Too preoccupied to notice her anxiety, he just stood there talking,

talking, talking, while she stared at him as though he were a ghost.

'Come on,' called my school friend suddenly, 'I've found my book. Let's run back to the lorry else they'll go without us.'

I don't remember if I worried about my mother during the long school day, nor whether I asked any questions when I returned home. Soon afterwards the image of the man in the woods gradually faded and disappeared forever. Or so it seemed.

It was nearly fifty years later that the memory of that encounter was reignited by Iain's story about Anton Kyphausen's visit to England in an attempt to talk to Churchill. Suddenly every small detail of that image was as clear as if it had happened yesterday.

15

Stockholm, a Nest of Spies 1943-45

Armgard arrived in Stockholm when temperatures had fallen to below freezing and people moved around the streets wrapped in voluminous layers of coats and boots and hats and scarves and gloves, so that it was difficult to recognise a familiar face. During her journey she carried in the depths of her clothes the incriminating letter that Richard Kuenzer had given her in Berlin. The first thing she did on arrival was to buy a stamp, stick it onto the letter and throw it in a letterbox. This was towards the end of 1943.

After an emotional reunion with Edzard and her parents, she settled into her new routine. Although there was now a restriction on the use of hot water, she had all the other day-to-day comforts she could only dream about during those long months she endured on her own in Berlin. At first she found it difficult to sleep soundly, since she was unconsciously waiting for the air-raid sirens to drag her from her bed and down into the damp basement. She also found meals a struggle; her stomach had shrunk to such an extent that she could only eat a few morsels of food at a time.

But by far the biggest hurdle confronting her would have been her new role as an agent.

It was a role that had no rules other than the penalty for not producing some evidence of activity, and which allowed her no opportunity to share her very real fears with anyone else. The slightest sign of revolt would endanger not only her own life but those of Edzard, her grandmother and Tante Sigrid.

After the war the Allies tried Walter Schellenberg, head of the German Foreign Political Information Service, AMT V1. Unlike other leading members of Himmler's team, he was spared the noose and given instead a six-year prison sentence. This was due not only to the fact that he persistently tried to broker a peace deal with the Allies - albeit not until he knew that Germany was on the road to defeat - but also because he agreed to testify against other Germans. He testified about many of those who had worked for him, including Armgard. A typed record was made of the short interrogation by the Allies that took place on 28th September 1946:

Question: *Who was Countess Knyphausen?*

Schellenberg: *She was separated from a journalist who worked in Sweden.*

Q: *Was she active in Sweden?*

S: *Yes, she worked for Finke in Sweden. Her work can be described as society gossip.*

Q: *Was she employed full-time or voluntarily?*

S: *She received money.*

●●●●●●●●●●●

Q: *Let us for a moment return to Countess Knyphausen. When did she work for you and how effective was she?*

S: *She worked for us since the beginning of 1944, if I remember correctly.*

Q: *The last half of my question was about how effective she was.*

S: *She did her best to give us insight into the political situation through reports on the Swedish society she frequented.*

Q: *How were her reports sent?*

S: *She left her reports at the German Legation.*

In early 1944, when Armgard started leaving her reports, the centre of Stockholm's espionage lay around the American Legation, which stood in a cul-de-sac just a stone's throw from the water's edge. In that same small cul-de-sac behind the Hotel Esplanade, Jacob and Marcus Wallenberg were busy running their banking and industrial empire while negotiating with both Germans and Allies. Next door to the Wallenberg offices stood the Gestapo headquarters and across an inlet of water - Stockholm is a series of waterways connected by fourteen islands - was the German Legation, where Finke worked.

Stockholm had become a teeming swarm of foreign agents

disguised as something else. Around the corner from the cul-de-sac where the Gestapo and the Americans worked was the home of an influential Danish spy who had a finger on every pulse; a few streets to the east, at Ridargatan 46, in an unimposing block of recently built flats, Henry Denham, officially the British Naval Attaché, was busily tracking down German ships. For a few months at the end of 1943, the Swedes arranged for two of their English-speaking agents to climb into the attic of Denham's four-storey building and lower a microphone down his chimney. Sitting patiently with pen and paper in hand, their duty was to note down every conversation and phone call he made. In his book, *Inside the Nazi Ring*, Denham recorded that after the war he read those reports and found that, though they were accurate on his movements and the names of his visitors, *'the veracity of the alleged conversations was somewhat imaginative'*.

Thinking that an attractive man like Denham might succumb to female charm, Swedish military contra-espionage also sent the wife of one of their officers to visit Denham in his flat, hoping she could persuade him to exchange information with them. When that failed, they sent the same lady to Falsterbo on the south coast, where diplomats spent their leisure time during the summer. However, Denham thwarted their plans yet again by failing to turn up.

Swedish Intelligence - known as the *Svestapo* - and the many foreign journalists and agents in Stockholm left no stone unturned to find any possible inside information on everyone else's business. Their work involved deception and cunning and also many opportunities for sexual adventures, since most foreign agents were in Sweden without their wives.

As the daughter of a Norwegian diplomat, Armgard was soon invited to parties all over town. Before long she was once again thrown into a circle of diplomatic life. Complete strangers invited her to parties, not necessarily because the hosts found her interesting or amusing, but because they saw her as the daughter of an accredited diplomat – and because acceptable single women were in short supply to even out the numbers around the dinner table. Armgard was grateful to have learnt during her younger years the art of asking questions in many different languages and listening with her whole concentration to the answers – or of making small talk without divulging anything of interest.

No one could possibly have guessed the terms she had accepted in exchange for getting her son and herself out of Germany. Not then, nor at any time later.

A two-page document written on 16th October 1946, lodged in the Swedish archives and marked 'SECRET', consists of notes taken at the British interrogation of Schüddekopff, Armgard's German-based boss in the *Sicherheitsdienst*. He described Armgard's work in detail, including this comment: '*Among her other best friends were [the Finnish] Field Marshal Mannerheim's daughter, and an engineer by the name of Graffman.*'

Holger Graffman, head of Swedish Naval Intelligence and Managing Director of AB Transfer, became something of a hero by travelling to Germany to secure the release of imprisoned Swedish workers who had been employed at the Match Company in Poland, and also for organising an operation that rescued Jews from concentration camps. Throughout the war he remained involved with American Intelligence. Armgard's connection to Holger Graffman came about through her longstanding friendship with his wife Julie – nee Hubrecht – who had been a close friend of hers in Brazil before the war. Armgard always actively nurtured friendships and had kept in touch with Julie ever since they partied together in Rio. It was only natural that they should meet frequently when Armgard was in Stockholm. This is an extract from the memoirs Julie wrote in 1995:

Somehow the war years loom much larger and longer in my mind than other years and yet it is difficult to write about them as one certainly wanted to forget about them as soon as possible … I never even kept a diary during the war as it seemed to me too dangerous.

Holger was very busy as usual. Stockholm was a nest of spies. This was quite interesting and exciting, he never told me anything about it then, but I heard a lot later.

We had many friends among the diplomats as well as in Naval and business circles, and on Sundays nearly always the house was full of people. Sometimes it was a bit complicated as, though I balked at ever having any Germans (and, later, Japanese) in the house, I could never feel unfriendly towards the Italians, Finns or Romanians. So we would divide the axis from the allies by having them on different floors and oscillate between them.

Armgard talked about those parties as one of the pleasures she enjoyed during her time in Stockholm. Julie never found out, even fifty years later, about Armgard's involvement with the

Sicherheitsdienst. After the war Julie visited Armgard in Switzerland and became a proxy mother to Edzard, inviting him often to her home in Sweden and her holiday house in Spain. Soon after her memoirs were printed, she sent a signed copy to Armgard with a hand-written dedication on the flyleaf: '*To Armgard, my oldest friend*'.

By virtue of her father's position at the Norwegian Legation in Stockholm, Armgard was once again considered a citizen of Norway and given a *främlingspass* – a Swedish visa for foreigners. Her bosses on AMT V1 were aware that her Norwegian father afforded her the perfect cover as their agent and therefore allowed her a long leash. Her duty to the *Sicherheitsdienst* was to write a report every two weeks, which she was to leave at an agreed place near her parents' apartment in Djursholm, by the Eddavägen tram stop. The reports were picked up by Dr Krüger, and flown by Lufthansa to Tempelhof airport in Berlin, where Ostuf Gippert, head of travel ABT V1 A5, usually collected them. Her code name was *die Gräfin* – the Countess.

The *Sicherheitdienst* cell to which she reported was established at the German Legation under SS-Sturmbannführer Dr Finke. A tall, heavy-set 38-year-old, with blond hair and grey-blue eyes, he was known officially as an assistant to the German Commercial Attaché, but he spent his days as an intelligence co-ordinator, keeping control of a disparate band of agents working for him in Sweden. Finke told the Allies after the war that he had complained to Berlin because Armgard's reports often went to Germany before he had a chance to read them. They were sent directly to

Schüddekopff.

This was because Schüddekopff did not want Finke to realise he was also acting as a double agent. Under interrogation after the war, he said that Finke asked Armgard several times to do work of greater importance, but she refused. He also told the Allies that in the summer of 1944 he advised *die Gräfin* to renew her relationship with 'the diplomat Noble' in order to make use of him to the advantage of the Hielscher opposition group, with which he himself had become involved.★

Some people in Stockholm were watching Finke carefully. In his book, *Touchlines of War*, Peter Tennant, the Press Attaché at the British Legation, who in reality worked as an intelligence agent for both SOE (Special Operations Executive) and PWE (Political Warfare Executive), described at second hand a conversation with a member of the inner circle in the Reich Chancellery. On 4th July 1944 he wrote this minute:

The man in question [the member of the Reich inner circle] ... is also connected with a certain Finke who appears to be a mysterious Gestapo agent in Sweden. [He] is said to be playing a double game and to be feathering his nest for himself and his friends in this country against the possibility of disaster befalling his Fatherland.

If everything Schüddekopff and 'the man in question' said were true, it becomes apparent that the tightrope Armgard walked was rising further and further from the safety net. She was in theory

---

★ Dr Friedrich Hielscher was a friend of Wolfram Sievers, with whom he had worked before the war. Hielscher later became involved in the opposition to Hitler and was arrested after the July 1944 plot.

working for all sides, but determined to give away no information of any importance to any of them and yet keep herself out of trouble by pretending she was.

Schüddekopff worked directly under Schellenberg – and Schellenberg was trying to organise a peace plan with the Allies through Sir Victor Mallet, the British Minister to Sweden. Himmler was also involved in these talks and agreed they should send their negotiator, the well-known Swedish businessman Marcus Wallenberg, to London to talk to Eden.

Himmler put forward a serious proposal for peace through Schellenberg and Wallenberg, but the British PWE in London chose to ignore it. The war carried on relentlessly.

Peter Tennant wrote:

We thought in Sweden that insistence on unconditional surrender prolonged the war, but we were in no position to view the whole picture as seen from London.

A few months before Armgard arrived in Stockholm a flamboyant Englishman disguised as an Assistant Military Attaché turned up to start work at the British Legation. His name was Ewan Butler, an undercover agent working for the PWE and its rival intelligence department, the SOE. He had instructions to work secretly with Sir Victor Mallet in his dealings with Schellenberg and Himmler, which allowed him a certain freedom of initiative while also reviving the activities of the SOE in Germany. Before the war Ewan had been *The Times* correspondent in Berlin, where he became a friend of Anton Knyphausen and dined with Anton and Armgard in their apartment and signed their guest book. He was also Paddy's first cousin, a fact Armgard never told me when we discussed her guest list. Nor did his name crop up on any of Anton's letters after the war. And nor did Ewan mention the name Knyphausen in his book about his role as an agent. I wonder why?

But in his book *Amateur Agent* Ewan does give us some light-hearted insights into his secret service role. As preparation for this work in Sweden, Ewan received a month's intensive training at Beaulieu Abbey in Hampshire. This included instruction from an ex-burglar in the art of entering homes, teaching him ingenious ways to 'case the joint' and how to cut duplicate keys from impressions made in plasticine. He was also taught methods of disguise; for example, how to use a little cigarette ash to change the look of his face, and the best way to alter his recognisable manner of walking and standing. At the end of the month he was sent to Arisaig in Scotland to learn about weapons and explosives.

One of the inventions he was shown by a chemist looked identical to the little gelatine capsules in which fuel for cigarette lighters was sold. These ingenious capsules did not, however, contain lighter fuel. Once pierced, they emitted a vile smell – a smell even worse than the concentrated essence of hundreds of pairs of dirty socks.

This glorious weapon could be pierced and squeezed into the pockets of German greatcoats, making them unwearable for many weeks. Ewan cheerfully ordered a generous assignment of them, knowing that German officers in Norway, where the SOE was busily helping the Norwegian resistance, were issued with only one greatcoat per man and that Scandinavian winters were long and cold.

He also put into his luggage some tins of the most up-to-date brand of itching powder, a concoction that would remain active on the skin for a long time after it was deposited there. This was used in Stockholm to put visiting German dignitaries out of action for a few days. Peter Tennant mentions in his book, *Touchlines of War,* that a complicated operation went into action at the Grand Hotel, close to the German Legation, where discreet relations were developed by British agents with laundry and bedroom staff, encouraging them to sprinkle the powder onto German guests' underclothes and bedclothes. In Norway, SOE volunteers packaged condoms that had been dusted with itching powder into German-Army-issue envelopes, ready for distribution to the troops.

Of course the SOE had its own secret printing establishment in the Legation, where the various agents could fabricate anything from condom envelopes to fake identity papers – or even invitation cards for receptions or dinner parties that never took place.

Stockholm was shaping up to be a rather agreeable posting for Ewan Butler. One of his assignments was to recruit German agents to send into Germany – people capable of sewing seeds of discontent among the locals and possibly even eliminating Hitler. His first attempt proved a failure. He wrote about it in his book, *Amateur Agent*:

Soon after my arrival in Stockholm one of the Legation messengers came to my office to report that a German was sitting in the lobby demanding to see someone on the staff of the Military Attaché.

'*He's a shabby little fellow, sir. Almost in rags, one might say. Says he's escaped from a concentration camp.*'

'*All right bring him up,*' *I said. This might be interesting in one way or another.*

We smuggled the man out of the Legation. The Swedish secret police, who kept patient vigil from a roadmenders' caravan permanently parked opposite our front entrance, may not have recognised the man who accompanied me to a taxi, since we had fitted him up with a hat and an overcoat ... Private Haas stayed with me for a week.

Haas talked and talked ... and there was no doubt that his hatred of Hitler was perfectly genuine.

We felt that Haas was at least a reasonable risk, and I suggested to London that Haas should be flown over for further interrogation with a view to his possible employment on a very dangerous mission indeed.

By 1943 the death of Hitler by the hand of a German would have altered the whole course of the war and history. Baker Street agreed that Haas should come to England, and one night, to his passionate relief, he clambered aboard one of our comparatively rare Dakotas.

The SOE in London eventually decided that on account of his past activities, the man presented too much of a risk and interned him instead on the Isle of Man, where he remained comfortably for the rest of the war.

Because of his special work with the Minister, Ewan had his own office in the Legation. He was helped there by Janet Gow, whose orderly mind, Peter Tennant suggests, produced a tidy office out of the chaos that would have resulted had she left it to Ewan.

In order to fulfill the obligations of being, in name at least, the Assistant Military Attaché, Ewan attended a string of dinner parties in Legations and private flats. These often consisted of anything up to twenty-five guests. After a hearty dinner there would be speeches followed by coffee, brandy and chocolates. At some of these dinners he would without doubt have met up again with Armgard and considered her a useful source.

She was thinner and considerably less radiant than Ewan had known her in Berlin, but he had every excuse to invite her out and talk to her about his family - and ask her about Germany. Since she had only just left Berlin, he would have been eager to find out about their mutual friends there. He needed reliable contacts.

Was he having a romantic liaison with her? Was he asking her to help his projects? Or was he involved in helping Anton, something he might not have wanted to discuss with Armgard? Whatever their involvement, their conversations would have been fascinating, each hiding their undercover role from the other. Their tasks, however, were not similar.

Whereas Ewan believed in his work and revelled in carrying it out, Armgard had no such safe base on which to stand. Every move she made and every word she uttered would have to be ingeniously weighed up and then delivered with the talent of an actor. She had to elicit from her companion some piece of unimportant information to pass on to Finke, while never allowing herself to mention anything, however trivial, that might throw suspicions on her own actions. The very fact that she had secured a meeting with a British Military Attaché would have impressed Finke.

However, she would also have to secure some useful knowledge to benefit Schüddekopff's peace missions, although she probably thought he was still handing her information straight back to the *Sicherheitsdienst*. Fortunately, unlike Ewan Butler, she never drank alcohol, so she would have been able to use her quick brain and much ingenuity to keep check of everything she said and heard. In Edzard's opinion, Armgard may well have enjoyed coping with the challenges that faced her, even though she knew danger lurked behind every door.

There was one person, however, she feared over and above everyone and everything else; should he ever find out the terms of her departure from Berlin she would certainly have found herself living on the streets at the mercy of both Allies and Germans.

That person was her father.

16

Anton Knyphausen 1943-44

Determined to play a part in the overthrow of Hitler and the restoration of a democratic Germany, Anton never rested in his attempts to win over the Allies to his way of thinking. While he was living and working in Finland he made many trips to Sweden, where he hoped to gain acceptance as a serious political player – and to work alongside the band of German dissenters who were living in Stockholm. They listened to him and to his story, but did not invite him into their inner sanctum. Noting that he was still writing for a German newspaper, they were wary of his authenticity as a trustworthy ally. They had good reason to watch their own backs and be careful of what they said, but the cold shoulder they gave Anton was heartbreaking to him and caused the beginning of a lack of confidence that was to haunt him in years to come.

Anton was still posted to Helsinki, travelling frequently around Europe and always handing in copy to the editors of his newspaper, the *Hamburger Fremdenblatt*. He wrote for a German readership, both in Germany and serving abroad, and found it necessary to consider the words of his articles carefully. In order to stay employed – and he needed to stay employed – he had to clothe his writing with just enough official jargon to satisfy the Ministry of Propaganda, while at the same time doing his best to report honestly and fairly what he saw and heard. He knew that if he allowed his editors to sense his passionate desire for a democratic Germany, he would be sent home and executed as a traitor.

As diligently as possible, he read all the statements made by Goebbels, the Minister of Propaganda, who was busy encouraging fervent nationalism throughout Germany. In an article in *Das Reich* in 1942, reviving memories of Germany's humiliation at the Treaty of Versailles, Goebbels had stated:

We are firmly convinced that the English and the Americans, and above all their Jewish rulers from behind the scenes, plan an even more grotesque intensification of what they did before - if they succeed once more in overcoming us.

His message worked. Most Germans were prepared to fight to the death for their country rather then risk the humiliation that they believed the Allies would heap on them if they lost.

Goebbels also threatened, terrorised and punished those who

chose to ignore his many instructions, which were transmitted daily to the public by way of the radio and articles in newspapers.

While Anton spent his days pondering how best to phrase his articles, Brita Gustafson, the lady for whom he had deserted Armgard, was working quietly underground to help Finnish Jews escape to Sweden. Having been born in Canada and raised in Åland, an island halfway between Sweden and Finland, she had many Swedish friends, and her work as a journalist for the American United Press brought her into contact with Americans in Sweden. Unlike Anton, she grew up with respect but little fear of authority, and had few qualms about doing what she thought was right, regardless of the consequences. They fed each other information and she used this knowledge to help a whole boatload of Jews escape safely to Sweden.

Anton met some of Brita's international friends and gained from them an insight into the direction the war had taken since the German defeat at Stalingrad. He did not pass on such defeatist stories to his readers, not only on account of the much-needed salary but also because it was important to continue his job with the newspaper which afforded him a precious Journalists' Pass, enabling him to travel to foreign countries.

By 1943 he was frequently on the move, visiting Sweden on several occasions, sometimes accompanying Brita on business trips for United Press, and sometimes alone on a mission for his newspaper. It was in Stockholm that he was able to pass on to the Allies his knowledge of what was happening in Germany and to tell them how he believed the war might be brought to an end.

In the Public Records Office in London there is a summary of a report he wrote while he was in Sweden. It is dated 7th September 1943 and was sent from the British Legation in Stockholm to the Foreign Office in London. In paragraph three, they quote Anton as saying:

When the chances of peace are discussed, people point out that a peace on the basis of unconditional capitulation is out of the question for the time being. The present government could not commit itself to this crucial step. Nor can the Government be overthrown, because there is no politically organised opposition in Germany. Terror and arrests are increasing daily. There are special courts for officers, and death sentences for the slightest sign of defeatism are already common. Among the higher officers there is a strong desire to provoke an upheaval, but after the experience of the Italian Generals, no one wishes to take the first step.

One of the senior Americans who listened to his opinion on two separate occasions was Abram Hewitt, Roosevelt's special envoy to Sweden.

'Please don't confuse Nazis with patriotic Germans who love their country and are thinking ahead to its future', Anton told anyone who would listen. 'There are many of us who are prepared to risk our lives to help get rid of Hitler. We need your help.'

In the Washington archives of the OSS (the newly formed Office of Strategic Services, the wartime intelligence agency that later became the CIA) is a memorandum marked 'Strictly Confidential', sent on 23rd March 1943 by an anonymous person at the American Legation in Stockholm. Only declassified in 2004, it is headed '*For Bill*', and begins:

Sunday afternoon, March 21st, 'the undersigned' [there is no signature on the memorandum] had a conference with one Anton Knyphausen.

The conference was held as the result of earlier overtures by Knyphausen to American Legation officials in Helsinki and Stockholm for such a meeting.

The gist of Knyphausen's ideas was that he wished it to be confidentially known that while he is strongly anti-Hitler and anti-Nazi, he considers himself to be a patriotic German. He claims particular American sympathies by virtue of the fact, he says, that his father is an American-born German and one of his grandmothers was also American born and, further, from the fact that his wife is the daughter of a former Norwegian Minister to Finland. [He had abandoned Armgard at this stage, but she was still legally his wife.]

It appears that earlier his thought was to seek a way to get to the United States but by the time of the conference, he was already committed to leave for Berlin at 9:00pm on Sunday and was to proceed from there to Paris in a few days, so that the earlier plan was nullified for the time being. Knyphausen is to go to Paris as the representative for the same group of papers he represented in Helsinki and says he believes this new post will be of a 'permanent' nature.

On being queried as to his motives for seeking passage to America ... he replied 'It is impossible to do anything in Germany at present for the overthrow of Hitler' and his hope was to get some place where he could work for such a cause.

He believes that while at the present time there is a large amount of radio propaganda directed at Germany ... it still remains 'enemy' propaganda to the German people ... and whatever promises of benevolence are contained therein are merely so much conversation, comparable to statements of Hitler, Goebbels etc.

The long memorandum ended:

Personally Knyphausen did not appear to have any particular part in mind that he wanted to have in the proposed Provisional Government … Physically he does not appear very strong and I am not impressed with him as a leader. However I do wish to credit him with giving a considerable amount of thought to his project. He is about 35 years of age and speaks English fairly well and appears to be well educated.

His subsequent visit to Paris that was mentioned in the memorandum was not, as Anton had suggested to his American interviewer, a permanent one – it lasted three months. None of the agents in Sweden seemed quite sure what he did during that time. He must have written enough articles to satisfy his editor, because he continued afterwards at his job in Helsinki.

He later told the Swedish authorities that he did not write political articles in Paris. Through the Czech citizen Maria Strossler, 24 Rue Barraul, Paris 13e, a representative of the Jewish underground movement in France, he was able to give out information about Jewish persecution. I believe Anton was more interested in holding on to his job and his relatively good life than becoming a martyr for a resistance movement. He professed commitment of a kind, but never quite managed to convince the Allies that he was worth cultivating.

He made several official visits to Germany from Finland during 1943. While in Berlin, he liked to visit his friend Lagi – the same Lagi Solf who introduced him to Armgard before the war and whose own wedding Anton and Armgard had attended. Now the Countess Hubert Ballestrem, Lagi and her mother, Hannah Solf, presided over an anti–Nazi salon – a group of friends who met for tea from time to time. While he was still living in Berlin, Anton frequently attended their meetings, which would became known in history books as the Solf tea parties or the *Solf-Kreis* (Solf Circle).

The group's main intention was to help people who were being persecuted by the Nazis. They arranged for many Jews to escape from Germany, but as a group they did not engage in subversive activities. Hanna and Lagi chose to keep a low profile; however, on 10th September 1943 a cleverly planted Swiss infiltrator, Dr Reckzeh, was brought unwittingly by a friend to a birthday party at Elisabeth von Thadden's home. He offered to carry letters for the group into Switzerland to give to their British and American friends – an offer that was gratefully accepted. Unfortunately for the assembled guests, Dr Reckzeh was an agent for the Gestapo. He handed over the letters to his bosses, as well as a list of all those who had attended the tea party. Himmler waited four months before he acted, spreading his tentacles to find yet more names associated with the *Solf-Kreis*.

In early November Anton happened to be in Berlin. He was making, in his own words, 'one last visit to Germany to see my elderly father and visit political friends'. It was on that visit that he received a phone call at his lodgings. The caller gave no name, but Anton recognised the voice at once; it was Wolfram Sievers, his old friend from *Wandervögel* days. He heard the voice clearly enunciating two words before hanging up: '*Hau ab!*' Get out of here!

Anton knew that Sievers now worked closely with Himmler. And he knew his friend was offering him a chance to save his life – while at the same time risking his own by making the call. Without even stopping to collect his suitcase, Anton fled the house, managing to board a train out of Berlin. He hardly dared breathe for fear of being recognised and apprehended, but good fortune stayed with him, allowing him to arrive safely in Helsinki to the welcoming arms of Brita.

Other friends of the Solfs were not so fortunate. On 12th January 1944 all the conspirators at the tea party, as well as those who were believed to be associated in any way with them, were arrested and imprisoned. After lengthy trials and physical torture, the suspected affiliates of the *Solf-Kreis*, including the hostess at the birthday party, Elisabeth von Thadden, were beheaded on 8th September 1944. All except for Hanna Solf and Lagi. Their lives hung by a slender thread.

Anton was living and working in Helsinki again. Armgard had reluctantly offered him a divorce so that he and Brita could be married on 2nd October 1943. Now that Brita was pregnant they felt it was even more imperative they escape from German-controlled territory. It would be relatively easy for Brita to leave Finland because of her job, but Anton was under suspicion and knew his every move was watched over by agents posing as German diplomats.

At the beginning of May 1944 he managed to make a dramatic

escape, helped by Baron Gösta von Uexkyll, a Swedish national and a close friend of Brita's.

The intelligence services of at least two countries recorded this hasty exit. The Finnish police sent this telegram to Washington on 10th May 1944:

The [Finnish] magazine Eteenpäin, without revealing its sources, tells that journalist Count Knyphausen, after deserting Nazi ideology has been handed over to the Gestapo by Finnish police before he survived to escape to Sweden. Police chief Anthoni acted as middleman.

The story is more dramatic as told in an American Office of Strategic Services (OSS) file dated 27th August 1944. I have shortened the account, which originally covered two pages.

After obtaining a Swedish visa and permission to leave Finland, Anton boarded a train at the station in Helsinki. He was approached by a policeman of the Finnish State Police who asked to see his passport. The official glanced through the pages and then refused to return it, telling Anton to go to the German Legation where it would be available for him to collect.

Anton knew only too well that if he went to the Legation they would not present him with his passport, but with a 'call-up' notice, dated one month previously, requiring him to fight for the German army in Russia. If he said he had never received the call-up, he would be labelled a liar and sent as a deserter to the front. Since the Legation was considered to be German Territory, the Finns could have done nothing to help him.

Instead of presenting himself at the German Legation, Anton made a dash to the office of an influential friend of his at the Finnish Ministry of Interior, whose name he refused to divulge. This friend organised a

Nansen passport with which Anton was able to escape by boat to Sweden. The policeman who had apprehended him was dismissed from his post soon afterwards under pressure from Gestapo agents in Finland. The unfortunate man, whose name was Kauhanen, was enrolled into the Finnish army and served the rest of the war on the Russian border.

Having achieved the near impossible, escaping alive from Berlin and then from Helsinki, Anton now faced a new dilemma in Stockholm. The Swiss editor of the *Thurgauer Zeitung*, who had offered him work, was now only prepared to pay for occasional freelance articles and Anton realised that his prospects of finding a full-time job in journalism were slim. He needed to start at once on the arduous task of endearing himself to the suspicious gathering of foreign journalists and spies who swarmed around the centre of Stockholm, and who would determine his future.

For the time being, Sweden was to be Anton's new home – a neutral safe haven away from the immediate grasp of the Nazis. He knew Armgard's parents had moved to Stockholm and supposed they would be living comfortably in an official Norwegian Legation residence. However, he guessed that although Omi might be prepared to speak to him and perhaps even offer help, Johan would slam the door in his face, not only for having abandoned his daughter for another woman, but also for being German.

What Anton did not yet know was that Armgard and Edzard were already living in Stockholm with her parents.

17

Anton, Armgard and Edzard 1944

These were confusing times for nine-year-old Edzard. He dearly loved his grandmother but stayed well out of Johan's way whenever he could. Johan was a strict disciplinarian who sometimes misunderstood the boy, causing them to be wary of each other. Nor was school easy. He had worked hard to perfect his spoken Swedish and yet the other boys still ignored him when they played games or sat down to eat, because he was still 'the German boy' in their eyes. And then, as if there were not enough other hurdles to overcome, Anton turned up in his life, making tentative steps to bond once more with his son. Edzard found him as frightening as his grandfather, although he was not quite sure why.

His grandparents lived in an imposing flat with one formal reception room, and a dining room suitable for entertaining large numbers. However, it only had two bedrooms. Johan and Omi occupied one bedroom each until Armgard and Edzard arrived, at which point Johan moved out of his room and slept on a bed set up behind a screen at one end of the main reception room, leaving his bedroom free for Armgard. Edzard slept on a sofa in the dining room. Some evenings, as the family sat listening to the world news after they had eaten their supper, acrimonious arguments erupted between Johan and his wife. Although Omi distrusted Hitler and all he stood for, she felt Germany should be allowed a compromise peace settlement and that it was up to the Allies to facilitate such a move. Johan adamantly disagreed. He loathed not only Hitler, but also the whole German nation for what they had done to his country. He would never forgive them and believed they should be firmly defeated.

Armgard and Edzard sat quietly, reading or doing crosswords: anything to pretend the conversation was not taking place but knowing there was no escape from the strident voices so sharply pitted against each other.

One evening the Michelets hosted a formal dinner party in their flat for about 20 diplomats and Swedish officials. Armgard was in attendance, helping her parents, and Edzard had been invited to join the adults, along with two other children of his own age. After dinner Johan made a pretentious speech in French extolling the Allies, which continued for so long that Edzard and his friends could not stop themselves from giggling at the absurdity of it.

Armgard looked at them sternly, ordering them to be quiet by placing her finger in front of her lips, but the children noticed that some of the other guests smiled at them and chuckled too, as if they also found the speech unnecessarily tedious; this started their giggling all over again and they buried their faces behind large linen table napkins to hide their laughter and hoped Johan was too engrossed in making an impression to notice their behaviour.

Meanwhile Anton was struggling to find work and enough money to pay the rent. He earned a small income writing freelance articles for the *Thurgauer Zeitung.* He also attempted to set up a European News Agency in Stockholm with Baron Uexyll; they hoped to provide subscribers with anti-Nazi information, but lack of funds brought that project to a halt. He wrote copiously: a manuscript about his peregrinations over the last five years, endless dissertations for circulation among expatriates and many articles for the Swedish press, some of which were published. He told agent 'A' from the American Legation that Gordon Young, who was on the editorial staff of the British *Daily Express,* was interested in receiving his articles. Also, according to Anton, a couple of days after he arrived in Stockholm Hugh Carleton Greene offered him a personal introduction to the BBC's Stockholm representative, Norman MacDonald. But nothing seemed to come of that either.

Still struggling as a journalist and eager to promote his ideas for an honourable settlement of the war, Anton would have made a point of contacting Ewan Butler at some stage, making every possible use of their earlier friendship. After all, he had information about Germany to offer the British agent in exchange for an opportunity to play some part himself in ending the war.

Rumours and innuendos were rife among the intelligence gatherers and proved provocatively easy to circulate. These pieces of fabricated gossip were known by English-speaking agents as 'sibs', short for *sibilare*, meaning hissing or whispering. However hard the agents tried to stick to the facts, there were of course times when these sibs were accidentally returned as 'reliable' intelligence information to London or Washington.

Many American agents were keeping an eye on Anton, trying to fit him into a neat category and failing absolutely. On 16th June 1944 an American known as *Saint* in Sweden sent a message to someone else known as *Saint* in Washington on the subject of 'Knyphausen, Anton, Graf'. This file was only declassified in 2006 and includes the following:

Subject is reported by reliable Danish and Finnish sources, to be a German 'plant'. His dramatic and conspicuous arrest on the train while attempting to leave Finland some time ago, plus his convenient escape, and also the fact that while supposedly in the German bad books he was granted a three month visa to Paris last year, indicates strongly that he is here on a very special mission for the Germans.

It is not yet decided what action, if any, will be taken in this case, but further developments will be reported.

On 20th July 1944 Colonel Claus von Stauffenberg, a German officer, made an attempt on Hitler's life. It went terribly wrong and many members of the group who planned the coup were rounded up immediately. In Washington, London and Moscow, governments broadcast the lie that those involved in the coup were merely Prussian *Junkers* (members of the landed nobility of Prussia and eastern Germany) wanting to preserve their power and property in an eventual peace deal.

Noel Annan, who worked alongside Paddy on the JIS in the Cabinet War Rooms in London, wrote about the failed coup in his book, *Changing Enemies*:

An appalling misjudgement followed when the BBC broadcast the names of those who might be supposed to be in the plot, leading the Gestapo to arrest several who had not been suspected. They were executed.

Those names had been given to Anthony Eden by members of the opposition themselves, who felt sure the British would help them in their mission, since many of them had solid British contacts.

In fact only a few of the German Resistance members were simply 'executed'; Claus von Stauffenberg was shot the following day in Berlin, but most of the plotters, who included Anton's brother-in-law, Richard Kuenzer, were taken to the infamous Ravensbrück concentration camp, where torture was a daily occurrence.

Meanwhile, in Stockholm Anton seemed eventually to have gained the trust of American intelligence. After the Normandy Landings even many top Nazis were becoming aware of the likelihood of defeat. In America, *Time Magazine* published an article on July 17th 1944 called 'Days of the Double N', referring to the German expression *Nach der Niederlage* (after the defeat), which included the following:

From Stockholm came the details of a weird Nazi plan to save Naziism after the war is lost. Count Anton von Knyphasuen, for years a German correspondent in Helsinki, said that he had decided to quit the Nazi cause, would gladly tell the Allied world what he knew. The Nazis, said Knyphausen, are preparing to use selected military units to form 'islands of resistance', chiefly in the mountain regions. They mean to emulate the Partisans. Headquarters will be near Berchtesgaden, where Hitler, Mussolini, selected quislings and lesser German dignitaries can defy the Allies from the Wagnerian Berghof. The radio will be used to guide a vast network of underground fanatics ...

Every German soldier must fight to the bitter end, Count Anton added.

Although the Allies and even some of his German fellow resistance members in Stockholm were unsure of Anton's loyalties, the Gestapo were absolutely clear about his anti-Nazi behaviour. Angry at his escape from their clutches, they resorted to *Sippenhaft*, the penalty imposed on the family of those disobeying orders. On 24th August 1944 they imprisoned his elderly father and two of his sisters: Hyma Benckiser, together with her husband Nikolaus, and Gerda Kuenzer, whose husband Richard was already in Ravensbrück Prison. The conditions in which they were kept were appalling.

Madelaine Oehmigen, Anton's youngest sister, who had once been engaged to Wolfram Sievers, was so upset by her family's fate that she asked Wolfram to pass a letter to Himmler imploring him to free her father, who was unwell. After some weeks her request was granted.

Deciding she would try to help once more, Madelaine wrote to Himmler a second time, explaining that she would be willing to change places with her sister Gerda, who had been sent to prison when her brother Anton '*von Finland nach Schweden ging*'. (went from Finland to Sweden)

Himmler replied to her letter on 16th February 1945, by which time Gerda had been imprisoned for over five months. He did not wish her to take her sister's place, but said:

Because of your big-hearted offer to change places with your sister Gerda Kuenzer, I will let her out, despite her husband's treason, as the rest of the family will be so loyal and faithful to their country.

Meanwhile in Swede an American agent, Volkerts – codenamed 'A' – met Anton on several occasions at the American Embassy. His comments were sent back to the OSS in Washington. Among them were:

27.8.44. Count A. G. von Kniephausen [sic] now belongs to the stateless category ... he claims to be on good terms with the revolting [sic] German Generals, and to have had previous knowledge of the attempt on Hitler.

On 3rd September 1944 'A' met Anton, together with Willy Brandt, who spent the war years in Sweden. Brandt would later become the West German Chancellor and win a Nobel Peace Prize. As a committed socialist, Brandt would have had little in common with Anton's conservative views. A file in the OSS includes this paragraph:

Both 'A' and Willi Brandt formed the impression that Kniephausen was a rather helpless and by no means dangerous person ... he will soon be able to place any information he may possess at the disposal of one of the greater powers of the United Nations.

By this time Anton had found lodgings in Sweden and was joined by Brita, who had given birth to a daughter on 19th September 1944. They named her Ida Maria after her Swiss-British grandmother, though she later became known simply as Maria. From time to time Anton fetched his son from the Michelet flat and they spent the day together. Edzard remained awkward and sullen, looking warily on the strange man who took him to meet another lady and her baby.

Anton was struggling to survive financially. In order to pay the bills he now worked as a gardener, delivered newly baked rolls on a bicycle to the shops in the early mornings, and accepted a job working with a group of expatriates in a glass-blowing enterprise called the *Svensk-Ungersk Glasskonst*. Edzard visited him at work and watched his father make colourful flowers or swans out of glass rods. He noticed that most of the workers' hands, including those of his father, were covered with seeping sores resulting from their burns as they twisted and shaped the red–hot glass over dancing flames. None of these men had received any training before starting work as glass blowers.

At the same time Anton still struggled tirelessly to promote his own ideas for the collapse of Nazism and wrote scores of reports for American and British intelligence, doing everything he could to keep his name constantly in front of the Allies

Peter Tennant wrote in his book about the war years in Sweden that he was very much aware of the frustration felt by the representatives of resistance groups at being used by foreign agents for nothing more than intelligence purposes:

Kniephausen told 'A' that there is a German citizen named Fink or Fincke employed by the German Chamber of Commerce. While still in Germany, von Kniephausen was warned that this man was a dangerous Gestapo agent.

Anton never discovered that Armgard was reporting once a fortnight to Finke. Such a possibility would not have occurred to him and he probably believed the same story about her departure from Berlin that she had given to everyone else. The thought that Armgard had been pressured into reporting to the Gestapo would have shocked him deeply, as he knew she was never a Nazi.

In March 1945 Anton published a book in Swedish, translated by his wife Brita. It was called *Tysk mot Tysk* – German against German. In the foreword Olof Lagercranz, a well-known man of letters in Sweden and a close friend of Brita, summed up the gist of the story by asking why, when you look at the strength of opposition movements in German-occupied countries such as Norway, was there not a similar concerted movement in Germany itself? The answer, he suggests, is that whereas Norwegians were prepared to help each other and take risks to undermine a hated enemy who had occupied their country, it was a different matter for the Germans, most of whom felt bound by a sense of pride in their country. The book did not sell well. With very little paid work, a wife and a small baby to feed, Anton felt undervalued and at times irritable. But he never gave up.

The American Volkerts still met Anton frequently. On 6th September 1944 a report was sent to Washington:

Anton von Kniephausen told 'A' that he is at present engaged in compiling a list of names of German journalists for 'the Americans' ... His continued sojourn in Sweden is only made possible on grounds of his representing himself to be the accredited correspondent of Thurgauer Zeitung, Switzerland.

And then in September 1944 Anton received a notice. It informed him that a public announcement from Germany had formally condemned 'the journalist Anton Graf zu Innhausen und Knyphausen' to death by hanging in Germany, whether or not he turned up at his trial on 31st October 1944. The net with which the Gestapo trawled for any remaining conspirators of the 20th July plot to kill Hitler had scooped up his name.

Surely now at last the Allies would listen to him and allow him to do something worthwhile to bring down the regime that was devastating his country and the world.

18

Buenos Aires 1945

In 1998, three of us sat together in Jennifer's London house: Jennifer, her father and me. Larry, as Sir Laurence Kirwan was known by his comrades in the Cabinet War Rooms, was stunned to hear that my mother had a sister living in Berlin during the war - and various German relatives. 'I cannot believe that your father had a German brother-in-law and that your mother had relatives fighting on the other side', he said. 'You know, we often wondered why Paddy was suddenly taken away from us at the beginning of 1945 and sent to Buenos Aires. We knew the war would soon be over.'

Jennifer Preston and I had worked together in London since 1980, and soon became friends. Only recently did we discover that our fathers had been colleagues on the Joint Intelligence Staff in Churchill's Cabinet War Rooms. In the early 1970s, when both men had retired, Sir Laurence used to dine with my parents at their house in Gloucester Square, in London. Now Jennifer had brought her father and me together.

'We always thought of your mother as Norwegian and knew nothing else', he continued. 'Nobody working with such high-level wartime secrets had German links. It would have been unthinkable. I remember once while I was working for the JIS I took on a new secretary. She was first class, but after she had worked with me for a couple of days I discovered she had a cousin married to a German. I got her out of the office that very day, telling her there was no way she could continue to work with us. I made her pack up her belongings and go.'

He paused to drink his coffee and reconsider what he had said. 'You know, the Foreign Office must have really wanted your father in that job, because they would have known about Sisi's German relations. I'm convinced nobody in the Cabinet War Rooms knew.'

He reminisced for a while, 'They were good days. We felt we were achieving something worthwhile. We were comrades. Sad for Paddy. He told me many years later how much he regretted not being in London to see the thing through.'

In one of the most crucial moments of British history, Paddy was a keeper of national secrets in the Cabinet War Rooms, working every day in an office almost next door to Churchill's. Challenged and fulfilled, he wished his father were still alive and aware of the position he held.

When his father died, Paddy inherited the baronetcy. Sixteen years later he was awarded his own knighthood by the Queen, as he set off to take up his post as British Ambassador to Poland. He used to tell us that he considered he had only done his job as a diplomat in many countries and never felt that that of itself was worthy of such recognition. 'On the other hand, the work I was most proud of was on the Joint Intelligence Staff during the war. We gave everything of ourselves and felt that through our efforts we were bringing the world a little nearer to a lasting peace. It was the best work I did in my whole life, but of course we weren't recognised for it; nor did we want to be.'

However, at the very end of 1944, just as victory was within the Allies' grasp and members of the JIS were working with renewed vigour to reach the finishing line, the Foreign Office told Paddy that he would be required to travel to Argentina early the following year to take charge of the British Embassy in Buenos Aires. They had a reason for sending Paddy Noble far away from London. It must have become apparent to senior members of staff in the Cabinet War Rooms that he had a German brother-in-law and, worse still, that brother-in-law was said to have come to England with the intention of talking to someone in a position of influence about making peace with Germany. Of course the German was sent packing at once, but the damage was done. Paddy could no longer remain a member of the JIS.

Before his arrival in Buenos Aires, the Foreign Office issued an order to its Embassy there, which ended:

As regards publicity you should issue no (repeat no) formal announcement concerning Sir A. Noble. But in dealing orally with enquiries, on Sir A. Noble's arrival at Buenos Aires you should insist that the appointment is a routine one merely.

It seemed that the Americans, angry with Argentina for appearing to side with the Germans, had withdrawn their Ambassador and asked the British Foreign Office to do the same. This would have left the British Embassy without anyone able to take charge. Paddy was, in the eyes of the American State Department, too senior for the job of Chargé d'Affaires, but the Foreign Office had reason to persist.

The revelation of Anton Knyphausen's appearance in London would not have been a surprise to Sisi, because he almost certainly went to find her in Surrey first, hoping she would lead him to Paddy. From that day on she would have dreaded the moment when Paddy found out that Anton had been in England.

Anton's visit to the UK probably happened in late 1944, when doodlebugs had mercifully ceased and there was a feeling in Britain that the Allies were nearing victory. Could it have been Ewan Butler who arranged for him to be flown into Scotland on one of the now more frequent transport planes flying out of Stockholm over the North Sea?

It would not have been difficult with his many contacts in Sweden, including Omi, for Anton to find out where Sisi was living. Once Anton found Sisi, he must have thought it would be easy to tug at her loyalty to Germany and to her grandmother, explaining that he only wanted peace with honour and an end to the killing. Sisi may not have known at that stage that he had deserted Armgard and he is unlikely to have told her. He had other, more important things to tell her, such as accounts of the horrific treatment that Hitler was meting out to dissenters – including many Germans whom Sisi knew. Anton knew that Paddy had made German friends before the war and spoke the language – he would surely listen now and be sympathetic to the good Germans, wouldn't he?

But of course Sisi herself had changed since Anton last saw her. And she knew very well that by now Paddy wanted nothing to do with a German plan for peace; he had often repeated Roosevelt's words to her, adding that it would be better for the future of world peace if Hitler surrendered unconditionally and then Germany could start afresh with the Allies' help.

I asked Iain to repeat to me his account of Anton's visit to England. He sent me an email on 18th April 2003:

As I think I told you, I first heard about Knyphausen's visit from Daisy [Daisy died in 1973] and later challenged Daddy about it. He had never discussed it. He confirmed the rumour and simply said: 'Knyphausen came to London when I was working in the Cabinet War Rooms, wishing to see Winston Churchill; there was great uncertainty about whether he had come as a spy or a friend, so he never saw Churchill and eventually returned.'

No more reliable information could be had than that, I would think.

'Anton never spoke to me about it,' Armgard confided long after the war, 'but then I suppose he would have kept it a secret if it was a failure, wouldn't he? My friend Count Toggenburg told me once that he heard a story about Anton visiting London to find Churchill. The Count was German, you know, with an American wife. I stayed with them once in Sweden after the war. He's dead now.'

It is interesting to note that although Washington has many files on Anton Knyphausen during his time in Sweden – some of which mention his contacts at the British Legation or the names of British journalists he came across – the Public Records Office in London has little about him in their archives. Were records 'pulled'? Certainly one file on Count Knyphausen in the Foreign Office Section is marked 'DESTROYED'. On whose instructions?

In her book, *The Unnecessary War. Whitehall and the German Resistance to Hitler,* Patricia Meehan writes:

The attempt [by the British Government] to silence the voices of the Opposition after the war is the greatest tribute that could have been paid to them.

On 31st July 1945 Paddy wrote a letter to Noel Annan, reminiscing about the work they had done together in the JIS during the war. In his book, *Changing Enemies*, Noel reproduced a part of Paddy's letter to him:

It was hellish hard work and often one was so tired that one could hardly think straight; but there was zest to it. We were at the centre of things and could often see the fruit of our work. What is more we were a happy band.

If Anton came to London using Paddy's name as a contact, Paddy would inevitably have been transferred away from 'the centre of things' and sent to Argentina. And is there a further twist to the story? Did the JIS, after hearing about Knyphausen's visit, have a moment of doubt about Paddy himself? Did they send him to Argentina, by now a hotbed of German spies giving secrets to the Russians, in order to test him?

Paddy, Sisi and their three children set sail for Buenos Aires at the end of January 1945. Our ship formed part of a convoy leaving Liverpool that had waited for more than a week in harbour until it was deemed to be the least dangerous moment to set sail.

Once at sea, Sisi held one-year-old Tim either in her arms or at the end of a pair of reins to deter him from crawling too near the edge of the deck, while Iain and I had the run of the ship. Permanently clad in life-jackets, we made friends with the crew, who took us on adventures deep down into the engine rooms and up near the bridge. We were not allowed to disturb the Captain at any time. He was busy with his officers studying the radar to monitor the whereabouts of German submarines, which hovered like basking sharks around us, eyeballing the convoy and waiting for an unguarded moment to attack. In the evenings we watched through a porthole as the Captains of Allied ships signalled from one to another with flashing lights. This was much more fun than going to school, and the excitement continued day after day. For the first week of the journey the passengers – there were barely more than a handful – practised lifeboat drill every morning. Iain and I clambered into our assigned boat ahead of our parents, wanting to laugh out loud at the fun of it all, yet somehow silenced by the sombre mood of the grown-ups. After the boat drill, the crew of merchant seamen handed round mugs of hot drink made with condensed milk and malt extract. It tasted delicious.

Once the convoy was well out into the Atlantic, away from imminent danger from submarines, the ships forked away from each other, every one of them heading for a different part of the Americas. When we finally arrived in Buenos Aires, nearly three weeks after leaving Britain, we were met by an Embassy chauffeur and driven to the Alvear Palace Hotel.

At breakfast the next morning Iain and I stared dumbfounded at our plates. We had been served a steak and two eggs. We had never seen a steak before, but we knew what eggs were; eggs were something to be treated with reverence because if you were very lucky you had one a week. Now, we learnt, we were to have two for breakfast each day, followed by toast with butter – as much butter as we liked.

This was to be our new life. We adapted. We were quick learners and needed to be. One morning, soon after our arrival in Buenos Aires, Paddy explained, 'We've arranged for you both to go to school. Iain will go to St Andrew's Boys School and Laila to Belgrano School. All your classes will be in Spanish in the mornings and English in the afternoons. You'll soon pick up Spanish.'

Although Buenos Aires had no shortage of food, petrol was rationed. So each morning the chauffeur stopped outside the two schools to drop us off, before continuing the journey to take our father to the British Embassy.

'Just remember to smile whenever the other girls talk to you', my father advised as the car drew up outside my school on the first day. 'If you keep smiling they'll want to be friendly, even if at first you don't understand much of what they're saying. You'll be alright, you know.' Somehow he always managed to give me that little bit of extra confidence I needed.

The family soon moved into a large flat on Avenida Alvear. The balcony, which ran the length of the main living area and dining room, overlooked trees on the avenue. It was an ideal room for entertaining large numbers of people. At the rear of the flat was a nursery wing with four bedrooms and a sitting room.

One evening when Tim was already fast asleep in his room and Iain and I were immersed in homework, Sisi brought a strange lady into the nursery, announcing, 'Come and meet your new nanny, Miss Palmer'.

She was old and plump. I followed my mother out of the room. 'Where's Peggy? I want Peggy to come back to us.'

She explained that Peggy was still in the WRENS, the Women's Navy, and could not rejoin us until the war ended; meanwhile they needed someone to look after Tim, as well as keep an eye on Iain and me whenever they attended official functions.

It was plain from the start that Miss Palmer and I would never be friends. Iain was older and came home from school late in the afternoon, so he didn't have to spend much time in the woman's company. Tim was too young to know better and seemed reasonably content to be bossed around by her.

Things cheered up at Easter. Argentine friends of my father's invited us to their *estancia* (large rural estate) for the weekend – without Miss Palmer. In beautiful countryside we rode horses and swam in a private swimming pool before sitting down to lunch. Out on the terrace a *carne asada* (barbecue) was being prepared and, after the beef was eaten, children and adults were given ice-cream covered with *dulce de leche* (a local caramel sauce). On Easter Day we hunted for large chocolate rabbits and solid milk chocolate eggs wrapped in coloured paper. Grinning with pleasure, we carried what was left of our goodies back to town and ran to put them safely in our bedrooms. We were overawed by so much chocolate; we had never seen such luxury and planned to feast on it in the next few days. But Miss Palmer saw our treasure and had other ideas.

'You're not used to eating chocolate. It'll make you sick. I'll keep it all in my drawer and give you one piece a day, which you'll eat on bread and butter.' She was hateful.

One evening Miss Palmer entertained a friend in the nursery. Before starting an intimate conversation with her, she should have noticed that I always kept my bedroom door open. With her slight Anglo-Argentine intonation, Miss Palmer was busy telling her friend all she knew about my father. Or rather what she didn't know. She felt sorry for him because he was so thin, all because the family were imprisoned by the Germans in China because he was a spy. It can't have been nice being British. A friend of hers, she went on, worked for the German Ambassador and lived in a proper Embassy, much better that this flat … but, she confided, those Germans will soon be defeated. And we want to make sure we're with the winning side, don't we?

In May the war in Europe ended. My parents invited a gathering of colleagues and friends to the flat to celebrate. They stood on the balcony cheering and rejoicing as a victory procession paraded down Avenida Alvear. I was allowed to drink as much orangeade as I liked. Noticing that my parents smiled all the time now, I felt sure they were excited for the same reason that I was: at last Peggy could come back to us and the dreadful Miss Palmer would be sent away.

Peggy in Buenos Aires after the war with Laila and Tim

19

The Reckoning 1945

Johan Michelet retired from the Norwegian Foreign Office just before the end of the war. He had always wanted to spend the remaining years of his life in Norway, but in view of Omi's German nationality and the loathing all Norwegians felt for their occupiers, they decided to settle in Sweden. They bought a large farmhouse called Klahammar Gård, outside Stallarholmen. The windows of the main rooms looked down over lawns towards Lake Mälaren, an inland waterway that flows eastwards for about 150 miles (250 kilometers) until it reaches the sea at Stockholm.

When Johan retired and left the city, Armgard left with him. Although the war had not yet ended, her bosses knew she would be of no use to them anymore, as defeat was imminent.

Johan celebrated the end of the war at Klahammar with Omi and his Swedish neighbours and cheered with heartfelt sincerity when it was announced that the Germans were pulling out of Norway. His country was once again a free and proud nation.

Edzard was happy at Klahammar. The spacious house afforded everyone their own bedroom and even a spare room for guests. He spent hours exploring the garden and made camps in the trees beyond the farm. His grandmother allowed him to help plant seedlings in her vegetable garden in the spring, and during the summer they wandered off together to pick wild mushrooms and juicy *blåbär* in the woods. Those tiny wild blueberries had a sweet-scented taste and an infinite capacity to stain anything they touched. Armgard laughed when Edzard returned from the woods.

'You've got a blue mouth and blue hands and even a blue shirt. Did you remember to put any *blåbär* in your basket?' Then she cleaned his face and hands and kissed him.

She had time to spend with him, often playing card games or helping him with his homework. Now that he was fluent in Swedish, he made friends at school, and when the sun shone he swam in the lake. Stockholm seemed far away and even his grandfather was less dour than before, so that they could sometimes have pleasant times together, raking the front drive or visiting the nearest town, Strängnäs, to buy newspapers or books.

And then in the beginning of October a demure Swiss banker turned up on the doorstep to disrupt everything.

Armgard explained to Edzard that the two of them had met

in Arosa and that they had corresponded intermittently since she came to Sweden. Edzard continued to run into the garden to be with his grandmother, ignoring his mother's friend.

To everyone's amazement, Armgard and the banker were married in Overselö Church some days later, on 10th October 1945, and set off at once for a new life in Basel.

With one signature on an official marriage document, Armgard relinquished her German nationality, her erstwhile surname of Knyphausen and her agent's name of *die Gräfin*. From now on she had Swiss nationality and her name was Frau von Gabain. As soon as they were married, her new husband asked Armgard to leave Edzard in Sweden for a year because his own mother, who lived in the interlinking flat to his, did not much care for children.

After the war Sweden had become anti-German and their police sided with the Allies in a meticulous search for anyone connected to the Gestapo. Because of this post-war attitude, Armgard had little choice but to act as she did. The Swedish Criminal Police Department were by now aware of her work for the Gestapo. The vengeful attitude of the Allies was palpable to anyone as internationally aware as Armgard; her father took not only Swedish newspapers but also read articles from the Norwegian press and discussed them with his family. She dare not risk being brought into the open until the clouds had cleared. She had done no harm, but knew that the stigma of her actions would blacken her name and that of her family.

Since she was living in Sweden on a *främlingspass*, she was particularly vulnerable. If she had not become a Swiss citizen through this marriage, the Swedes would undoubtedly have taken away her *främlingspass* because of her involvement with the *Sicherheitdienst*, leaving her with only a German passport. She had no wish to live in Germany, especially after hearing about the witch hunts being conducted there by the Allies against anyone with Nazi connections. She had no money of her own, and no home. Even her furniture had been destroyed by bombs. There was not one friend or family member who could help her out of the predicament in which she found herself.

This marriage must have been her only option.

Paddy would have received news of Armgard's involvement with the *Sicherheitdienst* after the war, when the Foreign Office informed him of what had been discovered at the interrogation of Schüddekopff. The captured agent admitted that he had hoped to use Armgard's 'close relationship to Noble'. He said he wanted to use it to help the opposition, but the Allies were doubtful and automatically disbelieved any such claims.

A Swiss Police report dated 21st January 1946 starts:

English sources informed us on 14th November 1945 about the aforementioned Frau von Gabain being a well known German confidante.

There is another letter, dated 21st June 1946, from The Criminal Police Commissioner Otto Danielson to the Chief of Bureau at the State Immigration Department, Stockholm. It is marked, in large black letters, 'SECRET'. The letter refers to

'Countess Irmgard [sic] Innhausen zu Knyphausen'. It states that she was an agent for the Reich during the war and that she handed her reports to Himmler's second in command, Schellenberg. It says both Finke and a public servant within the services of the Reich had confirmed this and suggested that her work was not particularly valuable – mostly gossip. It goes on:

The Allies are particularly keen that the results of this cross-questioning in Germany of these arrested Nazi-sympathisers should not be publicized; I would be grateful if these statements could be handled with some secrecy.

Was it Paddy who asked for her case to be handled with secrecy? Did he do it for Armgard's sake or his own?

When he told Sisi about her sister's role in Stockholm he was probably resentful, unapproachable. It must have been in Buenos Aires, sitting in their comfortable flat on the Avenida Alvear, that he suggested they should never talk about the matter again – for their own benefit and Armgard's. It was a subject best forgotten.

20

Defeat 1945-48

While citizens of Allied countries were busy celebrating a great victory in Europe and newspapers sang the praises of their gallant armed forces, they gave little thought to those civilians and soldiers who had the misfortune to be on the wrong side.

Only Allied troops who were still serving in Germany had their eyes opened to the truth, the important truth that wherever and whenever there is victory there is also a defeat.

For Berliners the undiluted horror of defeat began as early as the middle of April 1945, when an ominous rumble of tanks and gunfire could be heard in the centre of Berlin, coming from the east. One and a half million Red Army soldiers were crossing the River Oder, using the terrain as a playground for their soldiers to loot and rape as if it were their due. The German Army had killed many thousands of Russians and now Russian soldiers were taking revenge. News of the horrors sped through eastern Germany.

By then there was no doubt that Berlin would fall to the invaders and that on their arrival in the city the Russians would free all political prisoners.

Since Stauffenberg's attempt on Hitler's life nine months previously, Anton's brother-in-law, Richard Kuenzer was held in Ravensbrück concentration camp, along with many of the other conspirators. Here is an extract from Isa Vermehren's book, *Reise Durch den Letzen Akt,* written about her visit to the camp during the latter part of 1944:

> *One of the unforgettable figures in these first weeks [at Ravensbrück] was old Mr Kuenzer who was returned one day from the interrogation wrapped in a blanket. He had been so badly beaten that he lay in bed more dead than alive in the open cell, needing constant care. When I met him after that for the first time on the walk I was deeply shocked about this toothless being, old before his time. For weeks and months his face had that harsh demeanour which occurs in faces whose souls have suffered intolerable pain. These nightly beatings which had become the rule after the July 20th assassination attempt disfigured all the faces horribly - these mistreated people came for the walk the next day with blue swollen eyes and cracked lips but, and this was even more frightening, they had a shimmering expression in their eyes.*

After Ravensbrück the conspirators, including Richard, were taken to Moabit Prison in Berlin during the winter of 1944. His wife, Gerda, who had been imprisoned as a result of her brother

Anton's defection to Sweden, was now free again, thanks to her sister Madelaine, to Wolfram Sievers, and to Himmler, whom she despised. But although she was once more living in Berlin, she was not given permission to visit her husband. By the middle of April 1945, it seemed certain that all political prisoners would be freed by the approaching Russians.

On the night of 22–23rd April 1945, as Red Army tanks were pushing their way into Berlin, Richard Kuenzer and his remaining fellow conspirators were led out of their prison cells and told they were to be set free. Prison officials ushered them through the exit gate and led them past a wall on their way to what they believed would be freedom and their waiting families. Instead they were gunned down against the wall by a line of armed SS men. One of the prisoners was badly wounded and lay quite still, pretending to be dead. He managed to escape soon afterwards. He was the only one to survive the shooting.

A few days later, Gerda was summoned to the prison for the purpose of identifying her husband's body. When she came to visit Armgard after the war Gerda told her, 'I recognised Richard only by the pullover he was wearing and which I had knitted for him'. She never recovered from that sight.

The men who tried so bravely to bring the war to an end by attempting to kill Hitler a year previously, without help from their own people – or from the Allies – are now remembered with a sandstone memorial in the Dorotheenstadt Cemetry in Berlin. It is inscribed with words in German from the Bible (Matthew 5: 10):'Blessed are they which are persecuted for righteousness' sake:

for theirs is the kingdom of heaven'. Underneath are their names and the date of their death.

As the Russians gradually took over the capital during that terrible April and May, Berlin was inhabited mostly by terrified women, children and a few elderly men. They knew that no one would be spared by Russian troops as they surged into town. Word had spread quickly about the atrocities already committed when the Red Army crossed eastern Germany. Revenge is never sweet.

Tante Sigrid managed to escape the worst violence by taking precautionary actions. Some time previously their house had been destroyed by flames, the result of a nearby bombing. They now lived in a fourth-floor flat. As the Red Army approached, she asked neighbours to help her carry food and water to the loft above her kitchen. She climbed into her hideaway and the ladder was removed. For three days and nights the Russians looted and raped in the area, after which everything settled into a kind of order among the disorder. At that point Tante Sigrid descended from her loft. Soon afterwards her husband was imprisoned. Too frightened to stay alone at night, unwilling to leave the house during the day in case he returned, she walked to the next suburb each evening to sleep in a friend's house.

During those first weeks after the war there was no electricity or water so, like everyone else, Tante Sigrid carried a bucket to the nearest communal tap every morning. Obtaining food of any kind became virtually impossible; she survived on hope. Hope that her husband might eventually be freed and hope that Bolko, her only remaining son, still in Russia, might possibly be alive and return one day to find her.

Lagi Solf and her mother were still in prison in Berlin when the Russians arrived. Whereas their fellow members of the Solf Circle were no longer alive, they had survived through the intervention of the Japanese Ambassador, who had been a close friend of Herr Solf and his wife when they were living at the German Legation in Tokyo before the war. The Ambassador pleaded constantly on behalf of the two women. On 3rd February 1945 an American bomb destroyed the People's Court, where their records were held, so once more they were given a stay of execution. When the Russians finally reached the prison, all detainees were set free, but by now the two Solf ladies bore little resemblance to their former selves. During the fifteen months they had spent incarcerated, they had watched a succession of their friends and acquaintances, all of whom had been part of the group they started, being led to their death by prison officers. Both Solf women died young.

Meanwhile, at Stötterlingenburg Miriam and her son, Wolfgang von Lambrecht-Benda, paid careful attention to details of the partitioning of Germany.

After the surrender, a new pattern of lines was drawn across the map of their country. The Allies divided Germany into four separate zones: American, British, Russian and, eventually, French. It soon became apparent to the von Lambrecht-Bendas that Stötterlingenburg, though close to the Russian zone, had mercifully landed in British hands. Within days, British officers moved into the house, leaving the family to live in a few rooms of their own. The soldiers went about their business, leaving the owners to get on with recovering theirs. Miriam and her son shared whatever garden vegetables they still had with the officers and, though their lives would never be the same, they started tentatively to hope for a new beginning. But fortune turned her back on them in the cruellest fashion.

Only one month after their arrival, the British officers received orders to leave. They explained to the von Lambrecht-Bendas that Russia had decided that the demarcation line should have been drawn further west. Since everyone was doing their best to placate Stalin, it seemed sensible to concede to his wishes – whether they were right or wrong. And so the line on the map was duly deleted and immediately redrawn three miles / five kilometres to the west – just at the foot of the Harz Mountains. With one stroke of a pen, a few strangers round a table had catapulted Stötterlingenburg House, Miriam, her family and all those who had worked for them over many years, into the hands of the marauding Russian Army.

As soon as they heard the news, the young von Lambrecht-Bendas scooped up their daughter Inez and the few valuables they could carry. They called for Miriam, telling her to join them; they were setting off on foot, hoping to reach the British zone before the Russians arrived.

But Miriam refused to join them, insisting that as she had lived for fifty years at Stötterlingenburg, she belonged there and nowhere else. Besides, she told them, it was her duty to preserve the house for future generations. They pleaded with her to join them, warning her of the mood of Red Army troops and repeating stories of atrocities that had reached them during the previous weeks. But nothing would dissuade her from staying.

After fond and tearful farewells, the young family set off to throw themselves onto the goodwill of neighbours whose house had miraculously remained in the British zone. The home of these generous people already served as a refuge for many families fleeing from the Russians. Nevertheless, they found one room for the von Lambrecht-Bendas, which they gratefully occupied for the next two years, knowing they were lucky to be alive and have a roof over their heads.

Miriam remained at Stötterlingenburg, the house that for her was more than bricks and mortar; it was the custodian of her memories. Every corner evoked thoughts of the past and as she wandered from room to room she recalled memories of happier times. Those wondrous Christmases when the farm workers and their families were invited into the *salon*, which she and her daughters had decorated with a huge Christmas tree. While everyone sang '*Stille Nacht, heilige Nacht*', Kurt handed presents to all the children.

The dining room had been the setting for grand dinner parties of twenty or thirty guests; fine linen tablecloths and gleaming silver were laid out by the butler for their influential guests from the world of politics and the arts. Sometimes, after dinner, a chamber ensemble played the sonatas of Kurt's famous great-grandfather, composer and violinist, Franz Benda. Perhaps as Miriam sat listening to Benda's violin sonatas on those evenings long ago, the romance of the strings might have caused her mind to wander to another man, Freiherr Oswald von Richthofen, then Under-Secretary of Foreign Affairs and her lover.

Before the First World War, when Miriam's husband, Kurt, was in the habit of spending the winter months in Monte Carlo, chancing his money at the roulette table, Oswald Richthofen came from time to time to Stötterlingenburg by train. Approaching the estate, Oswald pulled the emergency cord and, being of considerable wealth, would place money for the fine onto his seat before jumping out of the train at the spot where a carriage from Stötterlingenburg awaited him. Miriam would be sitting in that carriage. Feechen, Omi's much younger sister, was his daughter.

Now, all these years later, as Miriam stood alone in her beloved home, she became aware of footsteps on the gravel. One of the estate workers had come running to tell her that Russian tanks were approaching the village. As she walked through the hand-carved front doors of the house, she fingered them once more as she passed, bringing herself comfort with the thought that one day her great-grandchildren – and their children – would admire them as they walked into the house. She waited on the front steps. From far off the rumble of approaching tanks vibrated through the air. Miriam was 82 years old. The lack of food over the past five years had stretched the skin over her bones so that at last she looked her age.

The noise of tanks grew louder and, as they turned through

the gates and rolled steadily down the drive, she walked towards them. The young Russian driver in the leading vehicle hesitated at the sight of the gaunt lady with her straight back. She held one hand in the air as if to halt him. He put his foot on the accelerator again. No one halted the Bolshevik Army. Certainly not a landowner.

Yet something caused him to stop just before reaching her. Whether it was her fearlessness, whether she reminded him of his own grandmother or whether quite simply he was tired of killing, nobody will ever know. After a few wordless moments he signalled to a colleague behind him, who climbed down and sauntered towards her.

The soldier had no difficulty scooping Miriam into his arms and carrying her to one side of the drive, where he laid her on the grass verge and stood guard while the tanks rolled forward.

Some time later an elderly couple from the village, one-time employees of the von Lambrecht-Bendas, found Miriam standing alone on the roadside. They escorted her to their cottage, where she stayed for the next eighteen months. Miriam's cousin, who lived nearby, starved to death, but Miriam's employees shared whatever morsels of food they could find with her, and in return Miriam worked for them, picking wild berries in the woods, milking their cow and doing household chores.

Fine houses were a new experience for Russian soldiers. They lived comfortably at Stötterlingenburg for a few months, using the toilet bowls to wash themselves and burning furniture to keep warm. They even boiled down the canvases of Wilhelm Gentz's paintings to recover a few drops of much-needed engine oil.

After the Russians left, communist administrators took over the house and ransacked everything that remained. They burnt Miriam's hand-carved front doors for firewood, ripped down curtains to use as bedding, shaved the wrought-iron balustrades off balconies and felled trees in the park for timber. Some time later they recycled the roof tiles from the church, leaving it open to all weathers.

More than a year after the end of the war, Miriam was given permission to leave Germany. She travelled by train and boat to Sweden, where she was able to spend the remaining year of her life with her daughter and her Norwegian son-in-law, Omi and Johan.

At her home in Sweden, Omi spent her days tending a large vegetable garden. Row upon row of gooseberries, raspberries, blackcurrants and strawberries were pruned, picked and bottled. Apples dangled from the boughs of trees and she even succeeded in growing such a prolific crop of potatoes that she harvested them when they were still small and served them with butter made from real cream. With so much luxurious food to sustain her, Miriam gradually regained some of her strength.

Johan suppressed his prejudices, making a valiant effort to welcome and even honour his German mother-in-law. Quietly in the early morning he stoked the fires, carrying wood to whichever room she was using. Once a week he made the journey into town for medicines to ease her pains.

Omi, although recovered from her earlier tuberculosis,

continued to endure stressful asthma attacks and still smoked a packet of cigarettes a day; they gave her temporary respite from the series of horror stories about the war that were still reaching her. Yet she found a new energy to nurse her mother.

Miriam enjoyed a peace of sorts. Always in charge of her own destiny, she walked round the garden each day and soon began painting watercolours, which allowed her to express her talents while at the same time calming the demons that lurked in her every thought. She died in her bed during the winter of 1947 and was buried in the churchyard at Stallarholmen. Before her death, news reached her that her daughter Sigrid had survived the terrible times in Berlin and was still alive, but that Bolko, Sigrid's only remaining son, had not returned from Russia.

Unlike his Western allies, Stalin did not send German prisoners home when the war ended. Thousands of German prisoners of war were forced into slave labour for many years after peace was declared. Amongst those soldiers was Bolko. Even fifty years after the war ended he was loath to rekindle those memories. He wrote to me in a letter:

Normally people who stood somewhere in a safe place are willing to talk about war. But I was at the front from the beginning and I hate to remember and to talk about it.

In 1999, at the time of Armgard's ninetieth birthday, he relented enough to speak of his ordeals as a prisoner. He asked me to meet him for a cup of coffee and to bring a notepad and pen with me, adding that he would prefer to tell his story in one go and not have to be reminded of those days ever again.

Bolko was captured by the Bolshevik Army in Bulgaria in 1944 and taken to Yelabuga in Kazan, where he was interned in a prison camp, joining a large group of officers who were incarcerated after the fall of Stalingrad (now Volgograd). Most of these men were still loyal to Hitler. When Bolko told them about the lack of order he had seen in Berlin when he was recently home on leave, and went on to suggest to his fellow officers that the war was as good as lost, they accused him of being anti-Nazi and a traitor to the Fatherland. Only later, when more German officers arrived at the camp, bringing the latest news from the front, did they gradually realise that they no longer had a leader to respect or a cause to fight for.

A huge fence surrounded their prison, which consisted of two fine old churches and a space between them allowing the officers room to exercise. Bolko was surprised to find that his prison had three kitchens: one to feed the officers, one for non commissioned officers and the third for soldiers. The soldiers lived in inferior quarters in another building. He soon discovered that Russian officers, even though they were supposedly communists and therefore equal, expected better food than their men. In the German Army Bolko and the other officers had eaten the same food as everyone else.

The vast majority of German officers survived the prison camps, but almost every soldier died. This was due partly to the better food the officers received – fish was plentiful in the Kama River nearby, a tributary of the Volga, so the officers lived on fish soup and bread – and partly because the officers were meticulous about washing themselves. They each had a ration of one cup of water per day for washing, but when winter came they were able to augment their rations by melting snow. Unlike the officers, soldiers succumbed to diseases such as influenza, which spread through their camp at alarming rates, and to a plague of lice.

The officers had one other advantage; they were blessed with their own military dentist and a female Russian doctor who visited from time to time.

After the German surrender in 1945, Bolko was given the choice of either staying in Yelabuga or transferring to a work camp. He chose to move on and was placed in a factory where breezeblocks were made. The following year, while he was carrying a large load of concrete, he recognised the face of a newly arrived fellow labourer. Coming closer, he found to his joy that the face belonged to a cousin, Hasso von Benda, who like Bolko was twenty-three years old. When the camp commandant discovered that Hasso had been a sculptor before the war, he put a stop to his work as brick maker and commissioned sculptures from him. Hasso quickly asked for an assistant and soon Bolko was also excused heavy labour to help make his moulds. With better rations and a more liberal regime, the two cousins provided the commandant with sculptures that he either sold in the marketplace or kept for himself.

A year later Bolko was moved to a coal-mining camp. For

two days he travelled by train; forty soldiers were herded into each cattle truck without being told where they were headed. From the station they walked for two days to reach a camp near the Dnieper River, where Bolko was set to work in a primitive coal mine alongside Russian men and women. A woman in her eighties told him that she worked in the mine because it was the only way she could earn enough money to live. A fine-looking and educated young Russian said he had been sent to the mine because his father, a leading military officer in Stalingrad, had voiced opposition to Stalin's regime.

In time Bolko was moved again, this time to a road construction site where many of the men who worked alongside him were Russians, all of them forced labour. The Gulag had already spread into every corner of the land and sucked in people from every walk of life. However terrible was his own treatment, Bolko realised that many Russians were faring just as badly.

And then one day he had an accident, breaking his leg. In hospital one of the doctors took pity on him. When his leg had almost completely healed, the doctor gave him walking sticks and instructions on how to fake a still-broken limb. He hobbled around the hospital until one day a guard instructed him to climb into a vehicle with an ex-SS German prisoner. With no idea where the two of them were being taken, they were overjoyed to arrive at a camp from where, they discovered, some German prisoners were being given a chance to go home. But first they had to pass a medical examination. During this procedure the doctor who was interrogating him about his injured leg slipped out of the room, so Bolko took the opportunity to study his own medical records. By this time he could both speak and read Russian, so he was able to read from his record that he had broken a leg but the ongoing limp was merely simulated. Hastily he pulled a razor from inside his jacket and scratched the offending words from the record. Terrified that the opportunity to leave Russia might be taken from him, he waited silently for the doctor's return. By good chance the man failed to notice Bolko's change to the document and soon he was loaded onto a crowded train heading west.

For the first time since his imprisonment in Russia the doors and windows of their carriage were left open – the Russians knew that their prisoners had no wish to escape. As the train carried them slowly through Russian countryside, Bolko saw women working in the fields, guarded by gun-carrying soldiers. The women shouted; he realised they were German and looked back at them with pity as the train left them behind. Eventually it stopped alongside a crowded platform where the name of the station was no longer written in Russian, but in Polish. The German prisoners were allowed to step down onto the platform, where Poles wanting to trade soon surrounded them.

'We'll give you bread if you give us gold fillings from your teeth', they called out. Some of the prisoners took a knife and extracted their fillings there and then in order to receive bread; both sides were pleased with the deal.

Finally they arrived at an exchange camp in Frankfurt an der Oder, which lies in Germany just over the border from Poland, where they were given clothes by the Russian administrators as well as 40 German marks and a three-day free travel pass written and stamped in German on one side and Russian on the other. Alas, the value of the mark collapsed that very day and the 40 marks became worthless, but the travel pass allowed Bolko to reach Berlin.

Although he had been given permission to send a telegram to his mother from the camp, she never received it. When at last Bolko arrived at the front door of his parents' flat, Tante Sigrid, thinking she had seen a ghost, collapsed from shock. After a wait of three long years after the war ended, she had finally assumed that, like so many other missing German soldiers, her son had died in Russia.

21

Wolfram Sievers' Trial 1947

Just when I thought I had gathered together all the threads of my research to make sense of Armgard's story, Edzard sent me a newly discovered letter, bringing Wolfram Sievers back into the foreground of my research. Now, as I read about the trials in Nuremberg and study Wolfram's letter, written when he was incarcerated there, I am reminded of the words I heard spoken in a school auditorium when I was about 15 years old.

My father was serving for two years in Finland and we lived in Helsinki at the British Legation, an elegant mansion house. I quickly learnt to travel by tram to school like everyone else, to speak Swedish and to enjoy a bowl of hot porridge for lunch each day. Finland was still suffering from post-war deprivations.

The school had a short religious service once a week, which sometimes included a sermon - or talk - from whichever church official was present on the day. One of these talks consisted of only a few sentences, yet I have remembered them all my life:

When you die and reach the gates of Heaven, you will be met by St Peter, who will decide whether you are worthy to enter. 'What good have you done in your life?' he will ask you. 'How have you helped other people?' It is the good in you that matters to Him.

In 1947, six years before I listened to those words, a panel of senior judges from the United States, Britain, France and Russia sentenced Wolfram Sievers to death for crimes against humanity. Under the circumstances, they had no choice but to do so. The good that Wolfram had done to help other people, risking his own life on several occasions for their benefit, was less important to the judges than the evidence of a letter showing his knowledge - and therefore his compliance - in an evil crime.

The trials took place at Nuremberg, a city reduced to rubble by Allied bombing, yet chosen for this historic purpose because it had the largest courthouse and prison still standing in Germany. After hearings that lasted for over a year, twelve top Nazi leaders were condemned to hang. Then the lesser trials, such as Wolfram Sievers', began. On 22nd April 1947 Wolfram wrote a letter to his friend Anton. He had already been in Nuremberg prison for well over a year and had been questioned in court by the British prosecutor, Lieutenant-Colonel Mervyn Griffith-Jones. Either Wolfram himself, or possibly one of his prison guards, typed the letter - written in German - entirely in large capital letters. The

letter is three pages long; I have taken the liberty of shortening it :
DEAR APPO,

... OUR FRIENDSHIP WILL SOON SPAN TWO DECADES ... IF I HAVE DONE A FEW THINGS AGAINST MY BETTER JUDGEMENT. I ONLY DID IT BECAUSE UNDER THE CIRCUMSTANCES IT WAS ONLY TO GET CLOSER TO OUR GOAL. I WAS ENGAGED AND INVOLVED IN THE OPPOSITION... WHO – UNLESS HE LIVED IT – KNOWS WHAT IT MEANS TO WEAR A MASK FOR YEARS, TO STAND BY THE HOMELAND AND THE TRUTH AND WHAT IS RIGHT, AND TO BE DISGUISED AS ONE OF THE ADVERSARIES IN ORDER TO COMBAT THEM BETTER? ... I CAN CALMLY LOOK INTO THE FUTURE SINCE THE COURT IS EXEMPLARY. MY OWN HEARING TOOK PLACE LAST WEEK ... THE BOSS OF MY [OPPOSITION] GROUP, FRIEDRICH HIELSCHER WAS A WITNESS. THE COURT FOLLOWED HIS EXPLANATIONS WITH GREAT SYMPATHY AND ASKED MANY QUESTIONS OF HIM. MANY ADDITIONAL EXPLANATIONS HAVE BEEN PRESENTED AND YOURS WILL BE ADDED TO THEM.

Wolfram went on to explain that after the unsuccessful 20th July plot to kill Hitler, he was brutally interrogated by the Gestapo on suspicion of being involved with Stauffenberg in the attempted coup. However, he managed to talk his way out of that accusation and retain his job as a Colonel in the SS, working for Himmler. While he was there he could keep eyes and ears open in order to inform his opposition group of what was happening at the command centre. Among the opposition members sent to prison after the failed coup was Friedrich Hielscher, his old friend. Somehow Wolfram managed to get him out of prison in December 1944 and, by enrolling him in the military, keep him out of reach of the SS. Hielscher repaid his friend by coming to testify at his trial in Nuremberg.

Wolfram had also saved Anton's life – twice. In 1943 he phoned Anton, warning him to get out of Germany after the Solf Circle was infiltrated. The second good deed, even more risky, happened soon after Anton reached Finland, as he describes in the letter:

LUCKILY THE DEPARTMENTS WERE FIGHTING EACH OTHER … THE GESTAPO BOSS MUELLER REQUESTED THAT YOU SHOULD BE ELIMINATED… AT THE TIME THE FINNISH POLICE WORKED CLOSELY WITH THE GESTAPO… WE MANAGED TO GAIN TIME WITH THE HELP OF SCHÜDDEKOPF AND MY PERSONAL GUARANTEE THAT YOU WERE NOT A SECRET CARRIER. THEN LUCKILY YOU MANAGED TO GET TO SWEDEN. HOW HAPPY WE WERE! BUT THEN YOU TALKED ON RADIO AND WROTE IN THE PRESS. AWKWARD FOR ME, YOUR GUARANTOR. IN THE END OF JANUARY I WAS SUMMONED BY THE GESTAPO … THINGS WERE STARTING TO FALL APART.

When, after the war, Anton heard that Wolfram was standing trial for war crimes, he wrote glowing testimonials about his friend and sent them to the *Justispalast* in Nuremberg. However, no amount of explanations and no amount of pleading could save Sievers from the gallows. He was brought before the court at what became known as 'The Doctors' Trial'.

Wolfram had climbed the ladder of his career until he was not only a Colonel in the SS, but also designated to be the General Secretary of the Ahnenerbe Society (Ancestral Society). In his book, *This is the Enemy,* the American journalist Frederick Oechsner, who lived in Berlin until the end of 1941 as head of United Press, described the Ahnenerbe in 1937 as a 'literal mania of Hitler's'. It was at first doomed to ridicule for its extraordinary anthropological research in Tibet and the Andes. Wolfram was brought in to raise money from businesses and banks to finance these expeditions; he was considered the best man for the job, being both charming and articulate. Later, when the British Navy made it impossible to continue research abroad, the work was carried on in Germany.

It was his role in the Ahnenherbe that brought Wolfram to Nuremberg. Although he was no more guilty than most of his colleagues, he was the only one sentenced to death, because the court had as evidence a letter he had signed ordering a collection of skeletons: Jews held in Dachau concentration camp were to be selected while still alive to provide specimens for the research. Despite pleading that he was legitimately involved in the opposition to Hitler, that he had done much to help members of the opposition escape the clutches of the Gestapo, and that that in order to stay in his job he was forced to comply with orders, he was hanged at Landsberg Prison in Bavaria, on 2nd June 1948, nearly a year after his sentence was pronounced.

His letter to Anton from prison contained this plea:
SINCE YOU ARE ONE OF THE VERY FEW WHO ESCAPED
EXECUTION, DESPITE THE DEATH SENTENCE ON
YOU HANDED OUT BY HITLER'S COURT OF LAW,
YOU OWE IT TO ALL THE MEN WHO WENT TO THEIR
DEATH IN GOOD FAITH AND WITH COURAGE TO BE
A GOOD CHRONICLER.

When he heard of his friend's death sentence, Anton had a
nervous breakdown. Perhaps it was the last straw in the series of
horror stories from Germany that were reaching him. He wrote
no articles about his life in the opposition during the war, nor
about any of his friends 'who went to their death in good faith
and with courage'. Even for a journalist, even for a man lucky
enough to escape a gruesome death himself, some memories are
too painful to relive.

22

The Burden of Secrets

This is the conundrum facing me. If Armgard's immediate bosses were all secretly working for the opposition, as Wolfram Sievers and Schüddekopf told the Allies they were, why did she feel the need to flee from Sweden into a hastily arranged marriage? Why not tell the truth: becoming an agent was her only method of escape from Germany. As an agent she had caused no harm to the Allies, in fact her immediate boss became a member of the opposition to Hitler. The man who offered her the job was also by then working secretly for the opposition. Surely the courts in Sweden would have understood that her method of escape from Berlin probably saved her son's life and that, because she accepted a role from the Nazis, she was able to do so without

Armgard before the war

committing members of her German family to incarceration and possible torture in prison. Armgard was articulate, personable and had many friends who might have come forward to plead her case.

I email these questions to Edzard. After a few days he replies:

Schüddekopf never told my mother anything, I believe. She was important. If someone got into the claws of the Gestapo they would beat you until you talked or were dead. It was most important that only very few knew anything. The more people knew - the more dangerous it got. My mother did not know Schüddekoppf was working towards the downfall of Hitler.

If she did not learn the whole story about Schüddekopf and Sievers until some years after the war ended, the news would

Armgard after the war, in a photo taken for her Swiss Police record, reproduced below

have come too late for her. By then she was married and living in Switzerland. What was she to do? Until then she had continued to tell the story of how she managed to get out of Germany, unnoticed 'because the Government Offices which housed all my papers had gone up in smoke, therefore the authorities had no way of tracing me'. Why change it all now and unmask herself as a liar?

There were other reasons for her to remain silent. She valued two friends in particular, her sister-in-law Gerda Kuenzer, whom she much admired, and Julie Graffman, in whose Stockholm home she had been made so welcome during the war. Might these two staunchly anti-Nazi ladies have felt betrayed if they had suddenly discovered her role as a German agent? Even if she explained to them that she only found out after the war that her bosses were working secretly for the opposition, she was lying to them during the war, when she still believed her bosses to be Nazis. Their husbands had trusted her completely. Would this new explanation leave Gerda and Julie confused – even angry? How could Armgard be sure, now that she was stranded in Switzerland?

And over and above all else, there was her father to consider. It would be almost impossible for her to explain that while she was living in his home in Stockholm, a home rented for his use by the Norwegian government, she had secretly worked for – and was paid as – an agent for the Nazis, even though in fact she was, as she later discovered, possibly working for the German opposition, without being fully aware of what was going on.

Johan never did learn about his daughter's method of escape from Germany. Edzard wrote:

Just imagine if he had known she worked for the Nazis. He would have been full of rage against her. He would have cut her out of his will and refused to ever see her again.

And what about Paddy and Sisi? Paddy knew about her role as an agent. It was possibly he who was behind the British Foreign Office suggestion:

The results of this cross-questioning in Germany of these arrested Nazi-sympathisers should not be publicized; I would be grateful if these statements could be handled with some secrecy.

Did she ever explain to him, long after the war was over, that her bosses became members of the opposition to Hitler? That she had saved her son's life by the only available method that would not result in her grandmother being sent to prison? Edzard told me his mother kept all the letters she had received after moving to live in Switzerland. When he went through them after her death, there were none from Paddy. If he had written a forgiving and friendly note she would have kept it - and she would also then have been invited to stay in the various large and comfortable Legations and Embassies in which he lived until his retirement in the 1970s.

Perhaps she guessed that he might not have believed her if she had told him it was never the intention of Sievers and Schüddekopf to get British secrets from him to help the Nazis. On the contrary, she could have said, they hoped she might allow them an introduction to British Intelligence. But she was probably aware that after the war the Allies were full of scepticism at the mention of Germans who 'professed to being part of an opposition group'. And indeed many of those Germans only joined opposition groups towards the end of the war, when they had enough insight to read between the lines of Goering's propaganda and realise that Germany was heading for an ignominious defeat. It was only many years later that stories of brave Germans started to be read and, eventually, believed.

What was Armgard to do?

We know now that she decided, rightly or wrongly, to bear the heavy burden of her own secret for the rest of her life, carrying on the strange new life in Basel that she had imposed upon herself. Like the writer she always longed to be, she rewrote the story of that difficult last year and a half of the war and started the next chapter as a new person. It was not long before she believed her own story.

Basel is Switzerland's second-biggest city. It lies on the borders of France and Germany and is blessed by the River Rhine, which carves a stately passage through the town from one end to the other. It is here that Armgard made her home with Kurt von Gabain after the war. They did not live near the river, nor in the attractive part of town splayed round the old city; they lived in an unprepossessing suburb not far from the tram route into town. To reach their flat from street level it was necessary to climb three narrow, curved flights of stairs to the front door. Although all of Armgard's furniture and paintings had been destroyed by bombs during the war and what little remained was stolen by the Russians immediately afterwards, she created a *salon* that rejoiced in a few good pieces of furniture inherited by Kurt, and some antique tablecloths subtly draped over anything of lesser quality. She managed to turn a pedestrian flat into a home with a touch of European old-world elegance.

However, no sooner had she settled in, only three months after her departure from Sweden, than she was summoned to appear before Berne's *Bundesanwaltschaft Polizeidienst*.

On 17th January 1946 Inspector Eberle faced Armgard and told her that the Criminal Police in Stockholm had asked for her to be sent back to Sweden for interrogation. In answer to their questions, she told them she went to Arosa simply for her son's health and did not report to the Gestapo while she was there. She did, however, admit giving the German Legation in Stockholm reports regarding the social life of members of the international community; however, the reports only concerned Swedes, Finns, Americans and the British.

On 21st January a notice was filed describing the interview; it ended:

As the intelligence actions admitted by Frau von Gabain took place in foreign countries and were directed neither against Switzerland nor its inhabitants, a punishable act is not met. Moreover the aforementioned has become a Swiss citizen after her marriage. Therefore there is no possibility of other sanctions against her.

She had cleared that hurdle, but others lay ahead.

When Kurt offered her marriage, which she hastily accepted, he told her he was descended from an aristocratic French family, then assured her he was well off, as he owned a block of flats in Basel, where they would live. All of which was true. He failed to add that he kept very tight control over his money, and parted with it only if absolutely necessary. And he was not fond of children.

When Edzard came to join his mother in September 1946, his stepfather treated him to a regime that went beyond discipline into what would now be deemed cruelty. This must have upset Armgard deeply, because a year or two later she asked her father if she and Edzard could return to live at Klahammar in Sweden. Johan refused her request, telling her that she had made her bed and must now lie in it. She did, however, journey often to her parents' home for holidays. To his great joy, Edzard was allowed to stay with his grandparents for the whole of his school holidays.

In 2005 he wrote me a letter telling me his impression of his mother's character after her second marriage:

Tennessee Williams wrote a play by the name of 'A Street Car called Desire'. In it Blanche, who was brought up on a huge plantation in the South, is living in the slums of New Orleans with her sister and her sister's husband - a brutal Polish proletarian. She is never really aware of her real surroundings. Like a dream she is still on the beautiful plantation with servants and luxuries ...

My mother had something of Blanche. I believe she was able to superimpose the film of her life as a diplomat's daughter in Peking and Rio on her reality. The present was a difficult passage - a difficult passage that made my mother stronger.

Luckily for Armgard the war was seldom mentioned in Basel, since the Swiss tended to find the subject awkward and best forgotten. Edzard suggests that Kurt discovered Armgard's espionage secret in about 1949 but kept it to himself because he also had a secret - one which could have hindered his career and the respectable standing he enjoyed in Basel. Armgard gradually made her own friends among the international community and became respected for her knowledge of the world and a command of many languages. Her life fell into a routine; every day at noon her husband returned from his office expecting to find lunch prepared by Armgard, whereupon he, his mother and Armgard, as well as Edzard if he was not at school, sat down to eat.

Her housekeeping money was strictly regulated, but after those years in Berlin under Allied bombs she was well accustomed to scrimping and saving every last penny and every left-over morsel of food. In her free time Armgard visited the Art Gallery, trawled second-hand shops for clothes or attended charity sales where she bought books. She read copiously in German and English and corresponded with her friends abroad, many of whom came to visit her. Lagi Solf and her mother came to Basel soon after the war; Armgard was happy to see them, and to listen quietly while they recounted some of their terrible experiences at the hands of the Nazis. Of course they were no longer the same gregarious and outgoing people she had once known and it was not long before both mother and daughter died.

Gerda Kuenzer stayed with Armgard in Basel on several occasions. They shared views on the tragedy of war and the Nazi regime, and Gerda lowered her voice to almost a whisper as she described to Armgard the horrors she had endured in prison as a result of Anton's defection from Finland to Sweden. Gerda never forgave her brother for causing his family so much grief when he chose to escape to Sweden. Yet had he not escaped, he would certainly have been put to death by the Nazis in the same brutal fashion as her husband.

Darling would have been more outspoken than ever about the horror of war. She also spent a few nights with Armgard, at a time when most people in Britain had nothing but distaste for anyone with German connections. She was housed in a spare room on the top floor of the building, and seemed impervious to the restrictions caused by the regime of stringency under which

Armgard lived. Once again she wrote glowingly in Armgard's guest book about how much she had enjoyed her stay; no doubt Kurt went to some lengths to charm her, not only because she was always amusing and outgoing, but also because she was, after all, *Lady* Noble. He liked titled people.

When Kurt's mother died, he moved into her bedroom in the interlinking flat. In time he inherited some money in Monte Carlo, where he bought two tiny studio flats, one for Armgard and one for himself. They spent a few months there every year. Armgard enjoyed meeting the international community at the British church and walking into town to attend afternoon concerts – her allowance never stretched to buying seats for the more fashionable evening performances.

She never questioned Kurt's right to run their lives, not even when he brought a young man to live with them in Basel who would, he explained to her, act as driver and handyman as they grew older. The man was given the top room in their building, as well as the use of a car and other gifts.

Constantly telling friends how lucky she was to find a home with Kurt in Switzerland, Armgard grew to believe her own story. After his retirement, he bought a small holiday house on the steep slopes of Lake Maggiore, where they worked together in the terraced garden, taking joint pride in their harvest of lemons and figs. Although he was homosexual, another secret Armgard guarded carefully, they created a harmonious relationship that benefited them both.

Well into old age Armgard looked after her health, keeping

Armgard in Monte Carlo
1996

her body trim with a series of exercises she performed quietly every morning before appearing for breakfast. Holding her head high, dressed in second-hand clothes, she remained steadfastly elegant, as if that on its own gave her the right to consider herself fortunate.

When Kurt died, Armgard was ninety years old. Indomitable to very nearly the end, even the stairs of the Basel block of flats could not conquer her spirit. Every day she descended to street level, walked around the block and then climbed the long haul up three steep flights to her front door. She carved a decent life for herself out of the poorest materials and kept her friends to the very end.

Only her relationship with Sisi was broken irreparably.

23

Paddy and Sisi

The war and its secrets played havoc with the relationship between Sisi and her only sister. It not only divided their loyalties, but left too much debris in its wake for them to start again. My younger son, Patrick, describes being in the London flat when Armgard came to stay with Sisi after Paddy died. It seemed to Patrick as though there were a rope of barbed wire between them so that, much as they would have liked it, neither could draw close to the other for fear of being hurt. Judging by their conversation and attitude towards each other, he felt sure it was mostly Sisi who kept that imaginary barrier between them so she could shelter behind it. I believe she unconsciously harboured a feeling of resentment because both Armgard and Anton had threatened

Paddy's job at a crucial time in the war, putting her into a position of blame.

By the time she was a widow, Sisi had managed to erase the details of wartime events from her mind, yet a vague feeling of shame had never left her. Her method of dealing with relationship difficulties had always been the same; growing up in an era before counselling and the therapy of talk had become the accepted method of solving such problems, she simply said nothing. Year after year she either ignored her sister's existence or pretended that nothing was amiss.

Since Armgard herself had no wish to be reminded of what happened in that last year of the war, the stand-off remained in place. They occasionally wrote each other letters – always in English, although my mother's German was still as fluent as ever – but those I read delved no deeper than the birth of their grandchildren or the sudden coming of autumn weather. Perhaps somewhere deep in her mind Sisi presumed that the mercy of passing time would eventually heal the wounds, but she had no idea how the process might start.

For the rest of his life Paddy used the Official Secrets Act as a cover for any wartime subject he preferred to avoid. Edzard was amazed when he realised that Paddy, who could so easily have spoken out, never divulged Armgard's secret, allowing her to live her own life as she herself determined. Neither Paddy nor Sisi mentioned Armgard's wartime work to Johan, to the Michelet cousins who stayed with the Nobles from time to time, to Edzard, or to anyone else. It would seem that my parents felt that the decision of whether the method Armgard used to leave Germany should be openly aired and in time pardoned, or kept tightly under wraps, had to be Armgard's choice and Armgard's alone.

'I understand', Edzard says, 'why they kept my mother's secret. But why did they treat me as if I had done something wrong? I never could understand that. It would have been better if they had given me some explanation – anything rather than the coldness I endured on my few visits to London.'

Edzard was working for an advertising agency in New York the very first time he met Paddy. This is how he described that meeting:

In 1958 my mother wrote me that Paddy and Sisi would arrive in New York harbor by the Queen Mary on their way to Mexico [where Paddy was serving as British Ambassador]. I had to wait a long time until they came down the gangway. I was worried to get back from my lunch break late. They said coldly hello then turned to the Embassy driver who led them to a car and took them off. They did not even look back.

My parents were obviously surprised to find Armgard's son standing at the bottom of the gangplank in New York, but surely they could have been more friendly. Edzard had done nothing at all to deserve such treatment. Did they fear that striking up a friendship with Sisi's nephew might compromise their need to forget the past? The shadows of war are long and cruel.

It was said of Sisi that when she lived in Rome soon after marrying Paddy, she was the life and soul of many parties. After the war she became a different person, bowing to Paddy's needs and tastes and showing a preference for being on her own in his

The Noble family at the Embassy in The Hague, where Paddy served as Britsh Ambassador from 1961-63. Seated l-r: Rosemary (Paddy's sister), Sisi and Darling (Paddy's mother) Standing,l-r Libby (Rosemary's daughter) Ernest (Rosemary's husband), Iain, Paddy, Kenneth Spence (Laila's first husband) Laila and Tim

company whenever possible. Gradually she gave up bridge and tennis, concentrating instead on tapestry or weaving, which she could do at home. Her love for Paddy never wavered, keeping her strong at all times and giving meaning to her life. They could often be spotted hand in hand, whether at a wedding, walking along the street or sitting in front of television.

Though nothing in his background had prepared him for

Paddy and Sisi in 1975 with their granddaughter Melanie Spence

the task, Paddy worked out for himself how to make a success of his marriage. Until the end of his life he openly adored his wife. Though he could be domineering and quick tempered on occasions, he was the glue that held them close; he made her laugh, he organised expeditions and adventures to keep the sparkle glowing and whenever a band started to play he danced with her, wrapping her in his arms. In this way, over the years, he became the greatest beneficiary of his own work. It was always evident to my brothers and me that although we were dearly loved, Paddy and Sisi put each other first in their thoughts.

During his last years, Sisi never left my father's side. She read to him when glaucoma took away his sight, made him comfortable at all times and arranged for friends and family to dine in their flat to keep him cheerful and entertained. After he died, her strength and will to live slowly disintegrated, so that I believe her own death came as a welcome relief.

At her request, she and Paddy are together now, in a grassy grave at the Noble family burial ground at the little church on the Ardkinglas estate. Surrounded by Noble family members and a profusion of flowers picked by Paddy's nieces, my son Patrick read a poem by Leo Marks, which Violette Szabo, the British Resistance heroine, used as a wartime code.

> *The life that I have is all that I have,*
> *The life that I have is yours.*
> *The love that I have of the life that I have*
> *Is yours and yours and yours,*
> *A sleep I shall have, a rest I shall have*
> *Yet death will be but a pause*
> *For the peace of my years in the long green grass*
> *Will be yours and yours and yours.*

23

❧

Anton 1945-97

Anton's life after the war was not easy. Still struggling to earn a living in Stockholm, unable to afford a car, he travelled by bus on expeditions to sell jewellery from door to door. Although he managed to earn a living of sorts for himself, his pregnant wife and his young daughter, he longed to return to journalism. Armgard was by now living in Switzerland with her new husband, yet, though Edzard was living only three hours by boat from Stockholm, with his grandparents, Anton seldom saw his son.

Edzard remembers Omi packing him on board a steam boat that picked up passengers near Klahammar to sail into Stockholm, where Anton and Brita met him. Resentful by then of his own mother, who had abandoned him, Edzard gradually became fond of Brita and his young stepsisters and looked forward to spending time with them. Yet he remained wary of Anton. He wrote:

My father was on one side a boheme, a romantic who was very curious about people and charming if he wanted to be. On the other side did father sometimes turn into 'the Count'. Full of cold anger. Destructive. And the change could come from one moment to the next.

After the war Anton was not granted permission to live in Germany. Firstly the British administration in Hamburg turned down his many pleas to return and start a new life in his own country. Did it have something to do with his abortive visit to Britain? While in Sweden he also attempted to obtain a visa to live in the United States, but had no success there either, staying in Sweden for another thirteen years. He wrote copious pleading letters to his many contacts abroad, meticulously keeping a copy of them. Two letters were sent to Hugh Carleton Greene, who answered politely, and one to Roosevelt's friend and secret agent in Stockholm, Abram Hewitt, whom Anton had visited twice in Stockholm. Anton reminded Hewitt about the time they had spent together and asked for his assistance in coming to America. The reply, assuming there was one, has not been found.

There is, however, no record of him having written to Paddy or Sisi. And although his many pleading letters were strewn with the names of contacts abroad who knew him or were related to him, he never mentioned the Nobles. I wonder why? He was, like most people, completely unaware of Armgard's role as an agent, so that would not have stopped him from contacting, or simply naming, Paddy.

In 1957, twelve years after the end of the war, Anton's father died and Anton inherited Remseck and some income from a farm in northern Germany. Only then was he given permission to return home and take over the running of what was left of the Remseck estate. He also managed at last to get back into journalism; for two years he wrote for the *Stuttgarter Nachrichten*, the principal Stuttgart newspaper. Together with Brita, he also started a small art gallery. By then they had four children; three daughters and then a son, Iko, who was born at Remseck. Some months before Anton's death in 1997, his daughter Susanne asked

Anton in New York in 1964 with his granddaughter Julie Knyphausen

him if he had any regrets. She was both startled and dismayed by the answer she received.

'My greatest regret', her father told her, 'is that I left Armgard.'

24

The Reunion 2005

In the late summer of 2002, three months before we knew that Armgard had accepted the role of agent in order to escape from Berlin, I paid my last visit to her flat in Basel. She was ninety three years old. Her arthritis made walking difficult and her mainstay, dignity, had begun to slip away. But her mind never faltered.

'My life has been interesting, but it's nearing the end', she told me.

'Oh no, you are still …'

'I am ready.'

Though she may at last have lost control of her once-healthy body, she still controlled the script of her own life. When asked if she felt fearful, she shook her head. 'No, I'm not frightened of death, because when it comes I shall be reunited with my grandmother.'

When Armgard was still a child at Stötterlingenburg and keen to learn, it was Miriam who opened her eyes to a world of art and culture; when Armgard was thought to be dying of the Spanish flu in 1918, Miriam lay beside her at night to give her the strength to go on. Miriam taught her granddaughter about courage and self respect when yet another war relentlessly destroyed everything they valued in their lives.

When I travelled to Basel in 2004, Armgard was in hospital. I was able to visit her once with Edzard and hold her hand. She died soon afterwards, confident that she would be reunited with the one person who understood everything.

At Armgard's request, Edzard carried her remains to Sweden. He and his family had rented a small cottage attached to Klahammar House, where the Michelets lived in their retirement and where Miriam spent the last months of her life. Not far away stands the small Överselö church. It was here, on 8th July 2005, that Armgard's life was remembered. The service was organised by Edzard, who met us outside the church with his wife, Renate, and his daughter, Julie – named after Edzard's godmother, Julie Graffman. My husband and I had flown from Australia for the ceremony and were greeted by a gathering of family members and friends. Soon we all quietly processed into the church, where the service was conducted largely in English for the benefit of the mixed nationalities who attended. Halfway through, the priest announced a five-minute silence, allowing time for each of us to contemplate Armgard's life.

By now everyone in that small church knew the role Armgard had accepted during the last year and a half of the war. What thoughts filled their minds as the silence grew more demanding? Had they, even in their own minds, answered questions that hung in the air? I cannot speak for them, only for myself. I had learnt much about the war during my research over the last fifteen years and I agree with the words written by Justine Hardy (about Kashmir) in 2010: '*The most lasting damage of war is to the mind*'. All wars leave lasting damage. I believe that had I stood in Armgard's shoes in 1943 and been offered that one chance to save my child's life, I would have taken it. But would I in later years have spoken out, admitting to the difficult role I had accepted, trying

The family united at Armgard's Memorial Service. l-r: Edzard, Iain, Julie (Edzard's daughter), Laila and Tim

to explain to a sceptical audience that I had done no harm? Could I have coped with the hostile reception this would have evoked from some family members and close friends? I don't know. Besides, I reminded myself, attitudes have changed greatly since 1945, so I was in no position now to assess the decisions she took immediately after the war. Instead I looked over to where the urn containing her ashes rested near the altar and wondered what heights Armgard might have reached in the world of journalism – or maybe as an internationally acclaimed novelist – if Hitler had not started a war.

As the memorial service drew to an end, the sun positioned itself immediately above us, its rays softening the façade of the old stone church and warming our hearts as we watched Edzard and Julie carry the urn across the graveyard. With great dignity they lowered it into Miriam's grave. Standing nearby, each holding a flower given to them by Edzard to place one after the other into the grave, were Edzard's German wife Renate, Julie's American husband Michael, my brothers Iain and Timothy Noble with their Scottish wives, Lucilla and Elizabeth, and George and myself. Alongside, among those waiting their turn to honour Armgard with a rose, were Maria and Susanne Knyphausen, the daughters of Anton and Brita, and John Graffman, the son of Julie who had known Armgard first in Brazil and then in Sweden. Despite what they by now knew, they had all chosen to make the long journey to bid farewell to Armgard and to honour her in this small country church.

Looking round, I saw my brothers standing shoulder to

shoulder with Edzard, their support for him palpable. In that moment I knew that the long cruel shadows of war, which for so many years divided our families, had finally been swept away.

The Knyphausens and the Nobles are reunited at last.

Can anything be more ridiculous than that a man should have the right to kill me because he lives on the other side of the water, and because his ruler has a quarrel with mine, though I have none with him?

Pascal, 1623 - 1662
from Pensées , translated by W F Trotter

Borders are scratched across the hearts of men
By strangers with a calm judicial pen
And when the borders bleed we watch with dread
The lines of ink along the map turn red.

By Marya Mannes   1904 - 1990
Rhymes for our Times